T0194801

A Survival Guide to Mental Illness

A Road to Recovery

The Silent Pandemic

BRYAN C. COREY

authorHOUSE®

AuthorHouse™
1663 Liberty Drive
Bloomington, IN 47403
www.authorhouse.com
Phone: 833-262-8899

Published by AuthorHouse 02/22/2022

ISBN: 978-1-6655-5219-6 (sc)
ISBN: 978-1-6655-5222-6 (e)

Library of Congress Control Number: 2022903184

Print information available on the last page.

This book is dedicated to all people who have a psychiatric diagnosis, people whose lives are cut short because of an illness, and people in the military who serve to protect our freedoms, come home with a condition, and need help to get their own lives back.

This book is also dedicated to children everywhere because I don't believe that a five-year-old girl with a psychiatric diagnosis should have to deal with stigma from her classmates.

It is also dedicated to all the people who share in the same dream that people with head trauma can be treated to recover from whatever condition they might have and live a quality life.

SUMMERY LIST OF CHAPTERS

PREFACE

The Spiral Staircase

When I decided to write this book, most of it was in retrospect of having lived through the experience of having a mental illness since I was diagnosed with schizophrenia at the age of nineteen. I felt a great need to share what it was that helped me to overcome this illness and thought this information would be useful to encourage others to do the same. I was besieged by breakthroughs and setbacks. In one instance, I had taken my medication early in the day and was supposed to board an airplane the next day. I was so exhausted and not coherent my mother felt like I should be observed at the hospital. While talking to the psychiatrist on call, I left the hospital, and the police had to be called to find me. I did not stay in the hospital, but this changed my plans to go to California the next day. In another instance, the doctors at Beth Israel Hospital in New York wanted to take me into another room to show other doctors that I was aware of my surroundings, could communicate, and was functioning higher than other people with my condition.

Initially, like most people, I knew nothing about the illness, its duration, or how it would affect me. I was subjected to psychoses, delusions, and lack of perception, physically and psychologically. Since this illness strikes most often when people are in their late teens or early twenties, I also felt the loss of my dreams and ambitions for my future life. Only others who have lived through this can understand the hurt caused by a mental illness. It affected me as well as my friends and family who believed in me. I was in a semi-comatose state through my younger years and did only menial tasks. I found that I was only wasting my time and that my goals for the future would never come to fruition.

Twenty-nine years later, I feel that I have emerged from doing battle with this illness, and my greatest hope is to give others the encouragement to recover as well. As one person fighting for the group, I also want to change the way these illnesses are perceived in the eyes of others. Overcoming the stigma of having a mental illness would go far toward enabling recovery.

WRITING THIS BOOK

I wrote this book, which is primarily about mental illness and a road to recovery, because I believe that everyone should have a fair chance at recovery rather than being limited to a life of illness. I deal with the discrimination first so that people can understand the cohesion of inclusive ideas in this book and in our culture, which is one of the things that we look at. The general "hush-hush" attitude toward mental illnesses is almost a monopoly. And the toll on the country is obvious. I've been at mental health institutions and in mental health groups in hospitals where I've talked to more than six hundred people over several years. Some of them had depression, bipolar disorder, schizophrenia, and other conditions up into their seventies and were still trying to find a medication that worked.

I've talked to over one hundred people with schizophrenia, and they are all, almost as a lot, catatonic. I've met military personnel sleeping on the sidewalks of New York City, trying to find someone who understands what they're going through or will just give them a helping hand. I've met people with depression who have tried every drug available to them and ended up using electroshock therapy, which was previously used to help people go from institutions back into society. I have met or known people who see psychopharmacologists and have been put on thirteen drugs at one time only to crash back into psychosis and have to start all over again. A great deal of the answers that come up in reading this book will shock you.

In history, we have beaten diseases that have had a massive impact on our populations, all the way back to the black plague, which wiped out two-thirds of Europe. That's not what scares me. Consider that we had the medications to treat people, and they were withheld from us. That's basically the situation with depression, schizophrenia, post-traumatic stress disorder (PTSD), and other illnesses. People are not getting the medications and therapy that can give them back their health. I was one of the many who did not get the knowledge about the medication that could make me better. After I did start to recover, I was asked by my psychiatrist to write about my experiences with the intention of putting pressure on the pharmaceutical industry or health-care system to get them to make the changes that we need to recover as a society. Just like anything else, you can buy your way out of a bad situation for $12,000 to $25,000 a week in a private institute, but I don't think that 99 percent of people can afford that. Getting into a private hospital is almost like being able to win in the stock market. Recovery is about getting the best care available, and it's expensive, or you're just lucky. It took me eleven years to get on the right medication that helped me.

If you look at history, there have been many plagues that people have overcome, like the coronavirus, and mental illness is our current "silent pandemic." There are still illnesses that we know little about. If you were given a choice to let one person live and another die, how would you make that decision? There are illnesses that can be treated, and we have a way to deal with them. I'm proof of that. I ask myself why and at what point mental illness was treated the way it was, slammed with tons of medications, and I can only find one real answer: greed. I was lucky to have a list of psychiatrists who were willing to share their information with me. And I'm indebted to them that my illness was treated to enable me to get to the place where I am now. But I don't think that we should rely on who's lucky and who's not, and these are the people I'm writing this book for—those who are not so lucky.

No one can predict when he or she will get a condition or a diagnosis of psychosis, which means basically a break from reality. It can happen to anyone in any situation. The list of people with a psychosis encompasses multiple diagnoses. Although I suffered from schizophrenia, which often includes psychosis, other illnesses like depression, bipolar disorder, dementia, Parkinson's, and so on can also have psychotic breaks. This does not justify stigmatizing them. Stigma is a bad form of alienating another person, putting someone down, or making derogatory comments about him or her, and it can, if not dealt with, throw monkey wrenches one after another that divide people and set people back from the goal of recovery. This can be very disengaging. Stigma is inappropriate and without regard for human values. It is based on ignorance and limits people from having the best possible outcome for their health. Finding the best possible way to the road to recovery incorporates a person having a safe setting and a support system. The psychiatrist or specialist is just the beginning of a support system. A support system that consists of people who will not alienate the person or discriminate against him or her is critical to recovery. I will be describing the ultimate idea of a support system later in this book.

If you are from the military and have been diagnosed with PTSD, if you have a concussion or have had several concussions from playing football or another sport, if you have had a neurological condition or were born with a psychiatric diagnosis, whatever the point of onset, there are many ways in our pain-oriented society to get a diagnosis. You are not alone. Sometimes you must reach out to others to help yourself overcome an illness. There is no price on life, and what you give tends to come back to you—it is reciprocity. Every day, you have a choice to help yourself and help others. No one makes it alone in this world. Also, you must realize there is a time to take care of yourself. As a goal, we would like to create a world that benefits everyone rather than a few. To give is to create an environment that benefits recovery. Statistics say that 19 million people in this country have some form of depression, one in a hundred has schizophrenia, and thousands of military veterans have come down with PTSD. There are three hundred types of psychiatric diagnoses listed in the *Diagnostic and Statistical Manual of Mental Health*, 2019, and hundreds of millions of people around the world who carry the label of having one.

In this book, I intend to show how certain groups of people are overlooked medically, undertreated, or never treated at all. I will give you all the information to treat and be able to overcome all these illnesses or benefit someone's quality of life. So, this book will devote itself partly to describing the dysfunction of the mental health system to its consumers, like the people diagnosed with depression or schizophrenia. Answers for this population have been well hidden from the sight of the families and friends of people with these illnesses. The science for recovery for many of these illnesses has been here for decades but underutilized

We have 46000 Psychiatrists to help 52.5 million People

There are 170,000 people "with disabilities" in institutions in the US from the date of 2014

Until the Silent Pandemic of Mental illness is out educated, and we are more informed

Get the best care possible and have the health and wellbeing that we all deserve

The Silent Pandemic

Will continue to be Silent

If We don't Rise up and Challenge our own, Demons That we face, 1/5 of this country will continue to suffer in Silence.

MY STORY, PART I

I was born in 1970 right about when Vietnam was ending. My parents divorced when I was two, and I moved many times when I was young because my father was teaching during the school year and working on a fishing boat during the summers. I was living with my father in the winters to go to school in California in the Los Angeles area and in New York City and Upstate New York through the summers with my mom and my older brother. I had several cousins in the Northeast and additional family.

When I was ten, my father, stepmother, brother, and I moved to a commune with seventy people in the San Francisco area. While my brother quickly went to school in New York to get a better education, I stayed behind with my father at the commune, where I remained for fifteen years. From 1980 to 1995, I did have opportunities to go to private school and work in a warehouse that I didn't take up, but I did know that if you had the means, you could benefit your life quite a bit or buy yourself out of a situation. I went directly from middle school to study at a university. Philosophy and communications were my study of preference. I later found out there was no money in it. I did have many friends and had the life of Riley on the commune, so to speak, since I could do basically anything I wanted to do. There were rules, but they were not enforced.

At the age of nineteen, I had the onset of schizophrenia, which was a psychotic break from reality. I woke up one morning and believed that I was hearing voices, which was extremely disturbing. I had seen my friend get hit by a car a day earlier. I was prescribed Haldol by the first doctor I saw, who was a private doctor. I had severe reactions to Haldol, meaning that I had a seizure at the commune and was very confused about my sense of values in life and what direction I was going in. I immediately went to a specialist, who took me off Haldol, which started the beginning of going forward with a list of medications, one after another. The doctor from the commune who was with me through this period said almost nothing, although he did call for someone's help to try to stop the seizure I was having.

My reaction was so bad that I felt I should have been taken in an ambulance to the hospital because of the severe pain that I was in. His advice was to not smoke and to have human contact. I couldn't believe that this was the science at the time. My experience of this was that I did not know the truth or what had happened to me. In fact, the specialist I went to first also told me that I "might" recover when I was about fifty-six or so.

After trying a list of medications over a period, I didn't feel that my condition was getting any better until I was put on Clozaril. When I was in my mid-thirties, I made a goal to be healthier in seven years and put forth every effort to out educate my illness, to get the best medication and the best care, and to use my time wisely. I attained all my goals because I wasn't willing to give up. Giving up is the only real reason not to be more informed or have one more day to look forward to being healthier. My best advice is to never give up.

MY STORY, PART II

At a certain point in my recovery, I realized that I had suppressed a very important incident in my past. At the age of seven, I had a three-hour dental surgery because I had bones growing on the back of my two front teeth. Unfortunately, during that time, when I should have been under or blacked out, I was awake and looking at the back of my eyeballs—a case of awake anesthesia. I was not out all the way. I was wondering if I would wake up or live through the surgery. I did hear that one in one hundred people die every year from a doctor's mistake, but at the age of seven, I don't think that I knew what to say or even understood what had happened. I finally knew how to explain it years later. I know that everyone gets an anesthetic when they get their molars out, but the neurological damage to my brain was horrific and became more apparent later in my life. I guess the point of this is that we might not all know the cause of our neurosis, or we may just shut it out unconsciously. I just don't believe in mystery. I'd rather have the truth, nothing less, nothing more.

The last several doctors who had opened to me asked me to write about what they felt was a dysfunctional system, and I made a promise to write about my experiences and what they have taught me. The bottom line is that there is no way to change the health-care industry or the system, but you can in many cases educate yourself and get your health back. My fondest wish is that all people with a diagnosis of mental illness find themselves an advocate, as I did, which has made the crucial difference in getting my health back. What had helped me in the past is that I knew that I had to get my situation straight in terms of where I lived and the environment that surrounded me. I had a difficult time making friends and networking. Looking back with hindsight, having friends and family in my life and being closer to psychiatric services made a huge difference. This didn't happen overnight, but at least I knew that I was on the right path. The bottom line is that this book is about the truth and all that I've found out in my life. I hope that you will find it enlightening.

REGULAR ILLNESSES AND HOW TO READ THIS BOOK

know that there are some "regular" illnesses that people have, like the cold or flu. I never knew when I was young that someone could die from them. The flu shot was always a good idea for me; at least I thought that it worked. In fact, there are so many diagnoses regarding mental illness that you just can't name them all. And these illnesses are in every country in the world; some are life-threatening and others not. Some are just cruel to live with and just do not go away. Fortunately, some are treatable or even curable, but brain injuries are the cruelest ones. You don't want to live with them. Consider breaking your femur and leaving it broken; there's not a real good point to that. Your brain is just a complex muscle with five senses of conceptual thought, but there's a lot more to having a healthy brain than you might think.

Unfortunately, understanding of this function of ourselves leaves more for your spirit than our understanding of the human condition.

It becomes difficult to keep your faith when you feel neglected. I mentioned before that I had taken nine of twelve medications available to me before I was given the one that works. Knowing that, I use nutrition, environment, a support system or family, and professional help.

Some people fall into patterns of repressing themselves. Denial, neglect, and isolation are not heathy. The goal is to not let that person feel as though he or she is being neglected.

If you're the main caregiver or just have surplus attention, it is well spent.

Psychology is a good tool to use, as therapy with another person. And certainly, call someone if you think that the person will hurt him- or herself or someone else.

I'm writing this book because of the care and devotion of my family and friends who have supported me to be my best and overcome the symptoms of the devastating illness of schizophrenia to be able to move on to a new part of what I know of as a healthy life. By writing this book, I hope to give the reader a view of everything pertaining to this type of illness, including the percentages for recovery and the best possible outcome. My goal is to bring a measure of science to human understanding, show all relevant aspects of the illness, address the person's symptoms, and talk about everything that has benefitted or hindered me through this long ordeal.

One thing I want to express through this experience is that everyone is different, and every individual expresses his or her own set of ideas. Each person needs to be understood on some level so that he or she may benefit from his or her environment, treatment, and personal goals. I hope that the information in this book will help readers to identify their own needs and develop those personal strengths that will show a way to achieve whatever they are meant to do. Although there are a lot of people today who have been diagnosed with a psychiatric illness, every case must be treated individually. Some treatment and medicine may work better for some people than others. In my experience, I went through many years without having the one drug that would have helped me the most, and I hope other people will not be subject to the same thing. What's important about this is that each person is able to find his or her individual care.

THE WORLD WE LIVE IN

If we had seventy-five people with broken legs in this country, it might be easier to treat all seventy-five with a cast than to treat one person with depression. And the difference here is that the brain is a complex muscle, considered to affect your intellect, motor functions, and whole neuroplasticity. While people with a diagnosis can be extremely intelligent, stigma still exists. HIV is a situation that we've all been dealing with for many years. In fact, 1.2 million people have been living with this virus. Consider the impact this disease will have not just in the United States but around the world.

And since the war on drugs goes on, instances of HIV, which also has stigma attached to it, will become more and more common. Even with better medication to help with it, the legalization of marijuana, which some say leads to the usage of other drugs, could be a contributing force to future diagnoses of mental illness. Medical marijuana may help in some conditions, like seizures, dementia, Crohn's, cancer, and others, according to ACE Medical Truths.com, but it is not necessarily good for a person who has a chemical brain imbalance because it can lower your IQ up to four points. Recently there's been a trend to believe that using marijuana does not contribute to the lessening of cognitive abilities, but I believe this is not a good idea for people with mental illness and can, in fact, set them back. All illicit drugs can play a role in or lead to the onset of a diagnosis, according to Dr. Miller of Rensselaer Mental Health. They can do irreparable harm to your mental health, the wellness of a functional mind, and cognitive thinking. There are a great number of designer drugs on the market, such as ecstasy, K-2, spice, and so on, and you don't know what they can do to your brain. All street drugs can do irreparable harm to a person by taking over his or her life or worse. In terms of recovery, I would stay clear of all street drugs since they can produce unknown chemical reactions and affect your brain for years to come. I would certainly not drive or operate a motor vehicle under the influence of street drugs or even some prescription drugs, especially when you have been warned against it. In our environment, you should be self-protective in terms of the people you socialize with and what you put into your body.

Since we've just covered drugs, the other source of mental illness is trauma. I had a break with reality when I saw someone hit by a car in front of me. Football comes first to mind, and we are getting new information about this issue on an almost daily basis. We are learning more information all the time. You can also have a neurological condition from birth, have a car accident, or have a sports injury, and so on, which can contribute to your getting a diagnosis of mental illness. We also know that if you are of Ashkenazi or Eastern European descent, it can be a precursor to bipolar disorder.

Neither did I realize that almost everyone deals with symptoms of one of these illnesses in his or her lifetime, but at age nineteen, I was diagnosed with, in my opinion, one of the worst afflictions that you can live with, schizophrenia. You really must have bad karma for that (reference to "My Story "chapters). And then I realized that I was not alone. There's an incredibly huge number of people suffering from these illnesses, and I saw all the illnesses that doctors must deal with. And in psychiatry, it's no fun ball of wax either. I was lucky to get the care that I needed in terms of medication, therapy, housing, and financial benefits. Changing your chemical balance does not happen overnight. I felt myself lucky to be treated at all.

DISCRIMINATION

The social injustice of judging people by their mental health tends to lead people to this idea that one person has less intelligence than another, which is far from the truth. When you look at a condition or diagnosis, people tend to put a label on the individual rather than looking at the whole person. I felt that after my diagnosis I was treated differently than other people who were in better health. At the time, I did not have a great deal of financial benefits. It seemed that wherever I lived, I was always playing by other people's rules.

Since I was in subsidized housing, I was assigned a supervisor and a social worker who would drop in at any time of the month to judge my habits or make a list of medications that I was on. I felt the difference between my circumstances and those of others who did not have a diagnosis. Having a condition has no relevance to your IQ. In fact, people who do have a condition can be more intelligent than others might think. Quite often, people will judge others to try to validate their own priorities and are far from understanding that a person, while reserved, may have far surpassed any criticism. Focusing on this idea, you may find it a good time to look at your surroundings and see whom you depend upon for support.

The environment that we live in and the labels that people put upon one another can create discrimination. People tend to sweep people up and put them in some category, not placing them where they will necessarily benefit. This is the beginning of a road that we don't want to go down. I feel that instead of putting a label on people and placing them in a box, we should consider creating an inclusive circle without discrimination. Stigma is an infantile way of putting a label on someone and just sets back that person's recovery. We know, in fact, that there are tens of millions of people with a diagnosis or condition in this country. In 2019, 52.5 million adults received mental health care, according to the National Institutes of Mental Health (NIMH). Unfortunately, some people tend to think or believe that they are above human values and principles and that they only apply to some. This misconception of these labels that we use just puts down others and is nothing more than bias without perspective or knowledge.

EVERYONE WILL NEED TO SEE A PSYCHIATRIST SOMETIME IN HIS OR HER LIFETIME

There are studies of children with developmental problems said to be due to vaccines, but this field of study says that this is untrue, up to this point.

If you don't have any precursors, such as concussions or trauma, the odds do go down. There have been some studies that show that your ancestors' lives might give you a precursor in terms of genetics. There is known to be a direct connection to getting bipolar depression if you are of Ashkenazi or Eastern European descent, according to Dr. Steve Sturges, a psychiatrist in Berkeley.

There are also things that might damage your frontal cortex or neural stimulators, like being exposed to chemicals or plastics. For instance, one of the new crazes is to use whippets, which is a form of nitrous oxide used to make whipped cream. And although people may think that they're harmless, they can do irreparable damage to your brain, including seizures, coma or even death, according to good RX paralysis. Nevertheless, when you do come to that point of getting professional help and you have survival information as to how to deal with your diagnosis, this book will give you information to help benefit you in recovery. The differences are that some illnesses, like Parkinson's or dementia, which there are now new medications for, do not necessarily meet the mark for treating the illness to the point of recovery but can help the quality of life.

In this book, we are focusing on the illnesses that we do have answers for, such as schizophrenia, PTSD, depression, and so on, as well as quality-of-life issues. Even though having to live with these illnesses can be crippling, to say the least, the problem with these and other diagnoses is that they are treated as alienating conditions. Additionally, I don't know anyone who has a condition or has a son, daughter, grandchild, or friend who does who will not need some help at some point in his or her life. These diagnoses affect not just our country but the entire world. Remember that the second- and third-world countries may have no system to treat these kinds of illnesses or difficulties.

With the benefit of knowledge and a system in place, there are special institutes that can give you the best chance of recovery. All our wishes are the same: to lead a healthy and fulfilling life. If you do study the information in this book, it will give you the benefit of being able to navigate our most confusing health-care system. After you do get professional care, you will want to study other topics. This includes tips about insurance, medication, nutrition, analysis, and how to keep safe and build a support system that works for you. Hopefully, you will be able to find the combination of knowledge to regain your health. Getting this knowledge can mean the difference in years of health or letting your illness consume the best years of your life.

MAKING A PLAN

At the beginning of your recovery process, you will find that a good, supportive environment with positive influences is a must-have for the continuation of your good health. Be aware that there are many people who will take advantage of someone who does not have many choices in life, which makes it doubly important to find a trustworthy advocate for yourself. Try to overcome judging and criticizing other people and feeling sorry for yourself. Ending bias and stigma starts with you. It is true that we should not judge other people until we've walked a mile in their shoes. I would rather choose to help another person to overcome an illness that is treatable than help someone judge or push another aside as if one life has more value or importance than another. Some people choose to discriminate against others rather than give them a hand up the ladder.

In my mind, this is because those people are projecting their own limitations onto others, and their own lack of self-love precludes them from offering a helping hand. Sometimes it takes only a small amount of energy to influence someone in a good and positive direction, meaning a part-time job, college, day groups, and so on. Most communities offer support groups for peers addressing social issues. There are again state benefits, some largely in big cities or urban communities, which will help with housing, although there may be a long wait list for them since the demand is so great and the resources are so limited. Having a condition does not mean that life ends—you can consider going back to school or starting your own business, both of which can be a big benefit for your future. When one person is going in a positive direction, other people can be very receptive to being encouraged to do the same and better themselves. Here is a list of things that can benefit a person or family in planning:

1. Get the best professional care that you can.
2. Create a safe and healthy place to live.
3. Be a part of whatever support groups there are in your area.
4. Get personal analysis or therapy.
5. Better your education.
6. Put your emphasis on creating a healthier life.
7. Have healthier relationships.
8. Benefit yourself financially.
9. Be in touch with community networking, such as peer groups and support groups from your local mental health clinics.

We must understand that it is our own baggage that leads us into making bad judgments about one another. Without realizing it, we make judgments about other people several times a day. Having morals is what helps us differentiate between right and wrong—it makes it easier to know what our values are, and those values are how we make decisions to set directions in our lives. If we give up our ideals along with our morals, we lose part of ourselves and compromise the glue that keeps our lives together. Sometimes judging others overcomes even our condition or diagnosis. We forget our values and fall into denial, closing our eyes to the truth. I believe in doing no harm and fighting against the demons who constantly want to win us over. If we let denial run our lives, then we live in a state of not benefitting ourselves or the people around us. We forget our purpose and our reasons for doing what we do. Creating a moral compass helps us to keep the focus on ourselves and helps us remember that there are better possibilities in choosing a future for ourselves and others around us.

HAVING FAITH AND STAYING POSITIVE

H aving faith can make a difference in a person's quality of life as well as help him or her to get healthy again. Just as people believe in one another, faith in ourselves can make a great deal of difference. If we realize that we have the power to influence other people to change in positive ways, we must acknowledge that faith can give us the power to recover or achieve things that we may not believe possible. I believe that people treated with love and regard can double or triple their ability to lead healthier lives. It takes so little to make a difference in someone else's life, but the trick is to get out of our own way and let the power of love heal. Believing in a higher power gives us a way to believe in each other. If we choose going down the route of denial, we give up on ourselves and others, and the rest of our lives go down too. Faith is believing in yourself and your well-being without compromise. Without it, it's hard to overcome the boundaries that we set for ourselves, which just makes recovery that much more difficult.

We all have good days and bad days. Dealing with having a condition or diagnosis is just as bad, if not worse, than dealing with regular day-to-day problems. There are basic needs that everyone has, such as food, water, your medications, and a roof over your head. Knowing that these are problems or obstacles with real solutions can be reassuring compared to not having a concrete diagnosis of your mental issues. Don't fall into the negative zone thinking about what you don't have, but keep your focus on solving those things that have solutions and are as important to your future recovery as getting a specific diagnosis. If you ask most people with a mental illness, they say they would give anything to be healthy again, yet if you give your day-to-day problems up, only to deal with your health, it tends to quantify the state of being that you live in. If there was no way to be healthier, some of us would throw in the towel for those day-to-day things, but know that every day that you go forward in your life and aggress on the idea of a healthier life, it's like killing two birds with one stone.

I once knew a man who had a diagnosis and lost almost everything in his apartment and had to be evicted because of a fire. He was able to say that he felt the universe was just telling him to move on. When you can stay positive, you are creating an opportunity to wake up and realize that what you have accomplished is a resolve of the fundamental nature of things.

RESILIENCIES AND PITFALLS

Some of us are more resilient than others. I was hospitalized nine times before I got my life back. No matter how much endurance or strength you have, mental illnesses can be very difficult to weather. There are ways to improve your overall state of health, which include medication, nutrition, control over your environment, and so on. Even if you take advantage of all these things that can benefit you, getting back to an optimum state of health takes a lot of knowledge and work. Then you must go through the duration of getting well and navigating the US health-care system. Those times when your health, well-being, and general state of consciousness seem to be in jeopardy, these are the times to use whatever support you can access. This is when the regular obstacles in your life seem to disappear against the sheer job of just having to take care of yourself. I call this the place of resurrection. This is a time to not necessarily go to the hospital but to get to a stable and comforting place.

One of my doctors once said some wise words: "Don't get involved with things that can be problematic." These obstacles don't have to be relevant to anyone other than yourself. Don't let yourself slide down when you can't occupy a level of consistency. Know that there are pitfalls in life that are meant to be there.

In the next three chapters, I'm going to describe all the things that I know of to keep yourself from going to the hospital, and in the last chapters, I will talk about the ironic difficulty of knowing that you are on a pathway to regaining your health. Only when you have the confirmation of knowing that you have resolved your health issues do you know that you have beaten the pitfalls or challenges as they come up. Don't feel bad if you must get help. Getting the help that you need is a better choice than living in a place where you can't see the positives in your life. Remember, there are always positives. Not having to go back to the hospital, which is a last resort, is a great assurance that you've been taking care of yourself in a good way.

NUTRITION

Since most diagnoses are from a chemical imbalance, there are ways to control the symptoms of a condition by using medication. First, you should know that a great percentage of my recovery is due to my research on nutrition, and I will share this with you to show you how you can be comforted by being in the zone.

When you're talking about nutrition, it is very underrated in terms of recovery. There are nutritional products that will help you benefit from whatever condition you might be suffering from. You might think that this is just a suggestion to help you feel more in shape, but nutrition can help build your mental capacity as well as help with the effects of some of the medications. It can also help with healing cell damage. This information is specifically food for the brain.

The following are health and nutritional products that I have benefitted from for my schizophrenia and continue to use today. There are different nutritional products that are suggested for each different diagnosis, and you can access these sites on the web.

First off, start with a regular men's or women's multivitamin. Fish oil has been known to make an extreme difference, and in my case, I feel the benefit of taking it as quickly as the next day. Turmeric, tea tree enzyme, niacin, and vitamin B complex (at least fifty milligrams per day) should all be included. And addressing the elephant in the room, please include a laxative if you need one since some of the antipsychotic medications will cause constipation. I once had to be hospitalized because of an impacted colon, which just shows you how resistant I was at the time to taking care of my general health.

Additionally, I believe in getting a flu shot every year (what do you have to lose?) and taking vitamin C on a regular basis, especially if you're a smoker. I was somewhat surprised to find that my doctors agreed with me about the importance of fish oil, as it has been carried down in my family that fish is one of the best nutritional brain foods out there. Do be careful as to which fish oil supplements you buy and read the labels since there are products out there that are substandard and won't give you the benefit that you're looking for. If you can't afford all these supplements at once, I would say that the fish oil is the most important in starting your recovery.

A

DEALING WITH YOUR SENSES

In terms of dealing with your senses, I would recommend three so-called tricks of the trade that will benefit you when your brain is working overtime. The first one is using ear plugs to keep out extra or unwanted stimulation. Once you've decided on the music of your choice, short bursts of easy listening can be very relaxing over the course of your day. My second recommendation is to be open to any Eastern practices like yoga, acupuncture, tai chi, and so on that can help keep you centered, give you a sense of peace, and help you focus on your goals, the main one being to take better care of yourself. Lastly, reading has always been a great way to relax and reset the body's functions. All of these experiences are designated to try to keep you in the zone and give you clarity and enjoyment as well as a way to collect yourself and heal.

One of the challenges that we all must face is leaving the safety of our homes and the bed that we sleep in every night to participate in the outside world. The first place to go is being with friends whom you trust. Initially, you want to make sure that you can be comfortable in other places. If you look at this experience as an opportunity to recreate yourself in a different environment, it may help you overcome whatever fears you have about leaving your comfort zone. Second, if you have supportive family members nearby, visiting for two or three days can be a way to rest and recharge your batteries to continue your focus of self-attention on recovery. You can schedule a planned vacation at a resort or on a cruise ship when you know what the amenities will be and feel that you will be comfortable with them. The comfort of being close to someone you love in a familiar setting can be beneficial to trying new activities that you might not do yourself when alone. And all these experiences can make you ready to travel to places further away, see new cultures, and form new ideas that will provide you with another way of looking at life differently. Making new judgments about ourselves and the world we live in can be life changing, and we may find that these new places, people, and things presented to us change what our real goals and obstacles are or may be. We have to keep an open mind if we expect to grow our dreams and aspirations. Remember that recovery includes healing not just the body but the mind and soul as well.

RECREATING YOURSELF AND PERSISTENT PROBLEMS

Recreating yourself is an asset. Actors do it regularly for every movie that they make. What there is to learn from this is that you cannot just put yourself in a box and not look outside of it. Some people think that we are on the inside looking out. I believe we are actually on the outside looking in. Being more extroverted and going out of your comfort zone is its own sense of vision. I have seen people change their name, their address, and their phone number quite easily. If things are not going the way you want them to, consider starting your life over, even if it means getting a new occupation or going back to school. The wonderful thing about New Year's is that we get to start our lives all over again. I myself moved from California to New York to start my life over in the midstream of my illness. If you surrender or settle into making a compromise in your life, that may follow you. The last thing that we want to do is be set into the old ways of our past. Don't let your illness own you. Remember that there are always answers to the questions that present themselves. Keep your head up. If you let your head hang down, you will be giving in to what future may belong to you. This means never giving up.

PERSISTENT PROBLEMS CONTINUE

We are all somewhat limited in one way or another. The obstacles in front of us do not always exhibit what we can do. If someone asks you if you can fly an airplane, for most people, the answer would be no because you need years of experience to accomplish that. The things we do are an investment in ourselves. Some of the things that we set out to accomplish take years upon years, such as getting a PhD. Life is trial and error. Let's hope that we can learn from our mistakes. Our effort is toward making goals that are suitable for us. There is a dichotomy as to when to focus and when to surrender. Don't bite off more than you can chew at any one time. Education is one example because many of our efforts are life learned.

After I got my health back, I was able to use the education that I had and the information that I learned from the doctors who had treated me to be able to write this book. I had never considered being a writer before, but it was an offshoot of my health care that led me in this direction. Just being a good listener in my therapy sessions led me to a future that I did not see at the time. If you can enjoy the things that you do and find your true calling, life becomes more enjoyable. We tend to resist those things that are not suitable for us. Our health, however, is a mandate. No one wants to be, or asks to be, mentally ill. In many cases, we resist our own goals of health even with the best care. If you slip into denial, your problems can persist. Embrace your health, and the problems will take care of themselves.

SOCIAL PSYCHOLOGY

I f you're reading this book for yourself, I certainly don't have to tell you how difficult having a relationship is.

When you have a diagnosis of mental illness, nonetheless, there is a lot of therapy and help available to you in the clinical fields, such as psychiatry, analysis, psychology, and therapy. We all do our best to get help for the situation that we find ourselves in. As social beings, it is important for us to understand the environments that we're all in as well as the elements that we deal with in a social sense. These personal or professional relationships are a large part of how people can engage themselves into understanding the dilemmas that you may face in a social society. First, I'm going to discuss a social psychology pyramid so that you can define it and create a structure and a plan to address people in this area.

Psychology rules. The foundation of this is that Rome was not built in a day, and our health is a marathon and not just for an hour every Sunday. This is inclusive of all your tools to be healthier. The rule to this is not to isolate and to play by the rules.

Make the following into a pyramid.

1. Foundation
2. Taking care of yourself
3. Abstract thinking
4. Keeping your appointments
5. Social regard
6. Conformity
7. Following the law
8. Participation
9. Social structure
10. Being able to respect and recreate the social boundaries in your life

DEFINITIONS

1. Foundation is being able to recreate your foundation around you to adapt and evolve.
2. Taking care of yourself is cleanliness, well-being, taking your medication, taking care of your surroundings and how you present yourself.
3. Abstract thinking is making your house a home. Taking care of your things shows that you have pride in who you are and what you have.
4. Keeping your appointments means that taking care of your health is most important.
5. Social regard—showing respect to the professionals who are taking care of you builds principles for yourself and others.
6. Conformity—we play by the rules of conformity because this shows us that we have a sense of regard toward others, and our agreements become more

worthy of who we are. We set these rules not just to benefit ourselves but to benefit our community.

7. Following the law gives us a respect for the idea of principles, which builds our values and morality and gives us an opportunity to create balance for the fabric that keeps us together as a country.

8. Participation—although a lot of us are socially phobic or impartial to others, we all share the same world, and our participation reminds us to not isolate or come to think we are alone.

9. Social structure—we all have some sense of a need to be recognized in some way, and it may seem impartial, though it is in the way that our causes are represented that others tend to notice what we give back.

10. Being able to respect and recreate the social boundaries in your life is about the need to respect others and be respected, which represents a fundamental desire to coexist and to cohabitate with one another. This may differ as our personal lives change and grow.

REFERRALS AND SELF-ESTEEM

I f you are concerned about your health on a day-to-day basis, like 99 percent of this country is, try to fit exercise, massage, acupuncture, and so on into your weekly routine. A day in the spa never hurt anyone. And don't be shy about taking advantage of any prophylactic tests that are offered to you. For example, if you wake up one day and you're having a panic attack, you can go to the nearest emergency room, and they will be able to address your concerns and determine whether it is a heart issue or a phobia.

When I went to the hospital a number of years ago, I told them that I was concerned for my heart and my breathing. They kept me overnight and tested me, and the tests showed that my heart was perfectly healthy and that my breathing rate and oxygen level were perfectly normal. These were two things that seemed to be most on my mind and that I could stop worrying about after this experience. Today, there are tests to show if you have a condition early on, like dementia, and treating something early gives you a much better chance of recovery or a better chance of quality of life.

You can't be too careful about your health. As much as we would like to predict the future and be in control of our own destiny, it's much better being safe than sorry. That means that taking a test in order for you to eliminate some worry in the back of your mind or so that nothing overcomes you or you do not wake up with a condition that you never thought you would have is a small price to pay. Don't feel alone.

It's almost impossible to not feel alone. And it's almost impossible at the same time to be alone. Which is to say that some people are more introverted than extroverted or the other way around. Sometimes no one wants to be alone, especially in terms of health, and no one wants to feel neglected. If you do feel as if you're in a corner or behind the eight ball, the best thing to do is to take some risk. Be willing to take one step at a time and include yourself in some social circle, which could lead to forming a future relationship. Get into a group that addresses the most pressing issues on your mind, whether they be loneliness, grief, anxiety, and so on. Some people just tend to connect better than others. And the one thing to remember is that you have nothing to lose and everything to gain.

Self-esteem is about feeling good about yourself, your accomplishments, and where you are in your own life. If you persist in comparing yourself to others and constantly come up short, it will only result in you undermining your self-esteem. I have talked about how important it is for your health and recovery to practice living only one day at a time and focus on positivity. Unfortunately, our minds and the prevailing culture trick us into looking outward when all we need to do is focus on ourselves. If you do the right thing for your mind and body, you will feel the positive energy. Being safe, strong, and aggressive in pursuing positive thinking can put you in a place of power.

The healthier you live, the better you feel. It is almost contagious. Others feel your energy and your good feelings. Feeling better enables you to confront obstacles with more energy, and the ideas that come from you go to others. It's almost like a merry-go-round of physics; once that positive motion starts, it continues to go forward.

We must remember that life is a precious gift, and if we take care of others, it comes back to us and vice versa. If you truly want to profit from life's energy, do something anonymously for someone else. Anonymity is great for the soul.

HELPING A FRIEND OR FAMILY MEMBER AND DEALING WITH OTHERS

I n this case, as in all cases, the best aspect of giving is when you expect nothing in return except getting the benefit of making another person's life better. This is one of the most generous acts that you could give yourself. I believe everyone is a public servant of some kind or other or just a giving person. Giving is a selfish act. Helping someone that you care about means giving your time, your energy, and your knowledge to another person regardless of the outcome. Someone told me at some point that generosity is our greatest strength, and I believe this to be true, especially when it doesn't cost you anything to give. The most interesting thing about how the world goes around is that when someone needs care, another person appears to fill that void. This is almost as if the investment is the fulfillment of the desire to raise another person up rather than push people away. Giving is the way to give value to the world and be the beneficiary at the same time. It is a real gift. This translates to a quality of life that changes us all.

You don't have to be a specialist to change the world. Just do it with one kind act at a time.

Apply the concept of paying it forward, whether it is just opening doors for someone or paying for someone's dinner anonymously. Whether you're related to someone or a friend or just an advocate of any kind, everyone who is willing to contribute can help. It becomes not just an individual but an entire community, changing the world that we live in.

Everyone tends to have his or her own view of life, meaning his or her own belief system, constitution, or values that make each person unique. Sometimes we only break through into these facets of others when we know another person well. I believe there is good in everyone waiting to be discovered. Sometimes those things tend to be submerged under the sand or unknown, and when someone shines a light into the world, it is hard not to notice even when things might seem to be dark or gloomy. We sometimes notice others far more than we give ourselves credit for. Often what we want to see in contrast is the value in other people.

As I was studying philosophy at a school in California, we discussed having your own point of view. I never really knew what this meant until I traveled to Hawaii and went up to one of the highest mountains to see a waterfall that was flowing in the background. Seeing this vision was very inspirational to me, and I realized what a true point of view was. We are the highest of peaks that we aspire to see in others, and we communicate to other people hoping to see this aspect in others as we see our own truths.

At the same time, knowing ourselves and acknowledging our accomplishments gives us perspective on the way that we relate to the world. The information we filter through and contribute to the world gives us an arsenal of regard and consideration to view the world with. In continuum, we see and relate to the world as we would want the world to see us.

TERMS OF ADVOCACY

I n some cases, it can seem very difficult to find a good advocate for yourself. The US health-care system just overlooks the total spectrum of individual health and seems to focus on the dangers of the environment, epidemics, new health crises, and so on. This does help protect each one of us in a broad way, but it still neglects to focus on an individual's personal well-being. If you are hospitalized in a mental health facility and deemed not to be a danger to yourself or society, there is generally a judge who is appointed so that you can advocate to be released from the hospital. This is where family and close friends come into the picture. They will be able to tell interested parties at the hospital about your history of mental wellness and possibly what circumstances brought on the current crisis. In my opinion, you should always give releases to the hospital to share your medical information with these personal advocates, if you feel that you can trust them implicitly and that they are only acting in your best interest. Despite the confidentiality laws, I think that hospital personnel are glad to get this information, especially when you may be in a psychotic state and unable to provide them with important information about your history. Having this information will ultimately affect how they plan a treatment program for you in the future. This may feel archaic.

If you are in a position where you have nowhere to live when you are brought into the hospital, there is a possibility that the medical institution may take custody of you if it's a question that your well-being is in present danger because of being destitute. Sometimes, to change your medication, it may be necessary to keep you under medical supervision. This happened to me when I was kept at Beth Israel Hospital in New York City for four months while they rotated medications every six weeks, trying to find the one that would work for me. They eventually settled on Clozaril, which, as I've said, started me on the road to recovery. Although no one wants to be in a hospital for the long term, you shouldn't fight it if you have even a small realization that you're not functioning at your best. It will be much harder to change medications once you go home; being supervised during that process is the best way to go.

When you are in the hospital and you are assigned a caseworker, it could be a great asset to you. This person is an intermediary between the hospital's policies and the outside world and should be your greatest advocate on the road to recovery. Although dealing with social workers can be tedious, they can play an important role in ensuring your well-being and helping with the transition from the hospital back into everyday life. They should also help to explain why certain procedures are being done and be able to tell you the long-term prognosis of your treatment. If you feel that they are not doing enough on your behalf because they already have too many cases, which unfortunately happens in our overcrowded system, do not hesitate to be the "squeaky wheel" and complain about your treatment. Again, if you are not capable of doing this for yourself, family and loved ones should do it on your behalf.

Since you may be incapacitated for a long time, having family have access to your doctor, caseworker, and social worker is extremely important for your recovery. This could make all the difference in whether you are put on a medication that works for you or sent home before you are fully functioning. And if you're not on the right medication, you could be destined to poor health for a long amount of time.

TAKING CARE OF YOURSELF
AND A PERSONAL LIFE

Although you may have a diagnosis of a mental illness, you cannot ignore the rest of your health. Pay attention to any other referrals your primary doctor may give you, such as to an eye doctor, rheumatologist, chiropractor, and so on. I know that it can seem that your whole life is taken up in seeing doctors, but if it must be this way, it must be. Use all the knowledge that you have put together concerning nutrition, exercise, alternative treatments, having a beneficial environment, and so on to raise your level of overall recovery. The joke is that you can suffer from major depression but end up in a car accident because you forgot to get your eyes checked. If your doctor tells you that you must go to physical therapy for a specific condition, take him or her seriously and make the appointment. Your overall health must be the ultimate concern, not something to just excuse yourself from because you think that one condition takes priority over another. Some illnesses may be more severe than others, but all can be made better over time.

Everyone has a personal life of some kind, married or single. Very often, we apply the adage of "the grass is always greener on the other side" when we consider our specific situation. What most people forget is that we must work on ourselves to create our own happiness; having another person in your life is not going to change that. What is right for some people may not be right for you at a certain time in your life. You should not judge your happiness against anyone else's. Being able to accept your current state of being in a relationship or not is a huge improvement over feeling sorry for yourself. If you find yourself constantly in the doldrums because you have convinced yourself that you're being shortchanged by life, it's good practice to go and talk to a professional. No matter what profession you're in or whom you may be attracted to, it's even written in the Declaration of Independence that you are guaranteed the pursuit of happiness. I've found it much easier to enjoy what I have rather than to always be pursuing something else that I think I may want. This paradox is something you can forget about but something that you will never give up.

A HEALTHIER LIFESTYLE

've lived in a lot of places in my life. Some have been the ultimate ride of an extrovert experience. Others have been quiet and peaceful. At a certain point in my recovery in 2014, I realized that for the money that it cost me to live in New York City, I could live Upstate like a king. Unfortunately, I initially became overwhelmed by the move and lost track of taking my meds. This resulted in a two-week hospitalization until I got back on track with my medications and was assigned a social worker and psychiatrist to help me get oriented in my new location. Since that was my last hospitalization nine years ago, I now think it may not have been such a bad thing since I got the help that I needed at the time. If you are considering moving for economic reasons, be sure to think about who will advocate for you and how you will be able to interact with the health-care system in a new environment. If you plan this out beforehand, it will greatly facilitate your expedition into unknown territory, which is something that I neglected to do. I would also suggest that one of the things that you do, if you move into a different environment, is to make sure that your ID and your insurance will relocate with you.

This will greatly help to facilitate things if you do need to be hospitalized.

Nonetheless, why not eat steak and lobster on the weekend and have a piña colada if it doesn't interfere with your meds? Nutrition must be important to everyone. Nutritious shakes are easy to make once a day. Learn to have a healthy diet and good nutrition and live the way that you want to. Get that maid once a month if you want, throw a party on the Fourth of July, take a dip in the pool. That never hurt anyone, but stay away from the deep end. I found I could live like this for nothing and start a savings account. You can do this several ways by taking Social Security early or taking advantage of disability, which might be offered to you. You could even rent out a room in your house if you're that lucky. Having a list of things that you want, especially for the simple things, can be a positive influence on your recovery. Positive thinking is a good idea but having it all and having the lifestyle that you want can be the best secret of all. Apply this to having the life that you want, and if you have just a little faith in yourself, beautiful things can happen.

A

A COUNTRY CATASTROPHICALLY ILL

As I said, there are a huge number of people with disabilities in this country. Nineteen million suffer from some depression, either mild, moderate, or severe, which is close to seventeen million people. Additionally, one in one hundred suffers from schizophrenia or schizoaffective disorder, which equals three million people. These are staggering numbers, not just because of the suffering but because of the severe pain and hardship that come along with these illnesses. All these illnesses are treatable, but not all of them are illnesses you can recover from. At worst, illnesses like dementia and Parkinson's can only result, if treated, in a better quality of life. Whether they are recognized as disabilities is determined by the label that people apply to them. If you look up depression on the computer, you will see a list of medications that are prescribed for that illness. And if you see or understand this population, you will see that they have a severely crippling condition. The use of medications is not only a way to bear the burden of their illness but to progress the pharmaceutical industry to ensure payments of a far reach. This is where science is separated from people's conditions.

We do have the wherewithal to treat and overcome some of these conditions. We do have the science to treat them, at least to the point where some people return to a good quality life and are monosymptomatic. Let me say that this information is documented and not easily found. Regarding developmental problems, such as autism, which one in fifty-six people now get at some point, if you don't catch and treat them at a young age, they are difficult to treat, as are conditions that arise later in life. Treating conditions early will play a huge role now and later in life.

With returning vets coming back from overseas, regardless of whatever label you put on these illnesses, the real trick is to be able to go through the system and be treated with the best medications available, because in truth, some will just not work as well as others. I do not believe that people should be treated as "sacrificial lambs" in the name of science. I would hope that the pharmaceutical companies would be able to put useful medications on the market before they have to pull them off the shelf. And why has no one ever equated the cost of dispensing ineffective medications to the social cost of warehousing an almost catatonic population? Is this the humane way to treat people who are sick through no fault of their own other than an unlucky throw of the dice in the gene pool?

I maintain that the people suffering from mental illness in our country have been completely shut out or overlooked in the compassion of their own peers. Americans have let stigma rule the day. Mentally ill people have been underserved as a minority and are being ignored and thought of as less of a priority in our society. Do we want to continue as a country ignoring the needs of the mentally ill and underutilizing this great percentage of our population? I hope that this book will help people with a mental illness diagnosis to beat the odds and find a way toward their own recovery. I hope, in my own small way, that writing this book will help some people to find their path forward, especially when some of them have returned from serving overseas to defend our freedoms and liberties.

This book was meant to educate people and get them the right information to recover instead of having a condition that is interpreted as a lifelong sentence.

THE WAY THE PHARMACEUTICAL INDUSTRY WORKS

The pharmaceutical companies put a new drug up for trial. The main watchdog for the pharmaceutical companies is the Center for Drug Evaluation and Research (CDER), whose job it is to evaluate new drugs before they can be sold on the market and provide information for doctors and patients to use medicine wisely. They make sure their benefits outweigh the risks. After they approve of a medication and deem it ready for the marketplace, they send it to the Food and Drug Administration (FDA) for consideration. Also, there is another set of ideas that say that the FDA regulations are being abused to get drugs marketed. Less effective and more dangerous drugs with adverse side effects are making it onto the market, putting consumers at risk at a much greater rate than thought. The problem is said to be that corruption of research by the pharmaceutical industries is key in flooding the market with less effective, more expensive drugs. According to America Today, what they don't tell you is that all these medications have side effects that they themselves might not know about and that these medications might later be pulled off the market because of these side effects. Take Risperdal, for example, which was found to cause breast tissue growth in men. Now here's the issue. If, after ten years of trial, they still do not know that these medications can lead to health problems, I would think that that's an extreme oversight. But if they did know after ten years that these side effects would lead to problems for the consumer and still put the drug on the market, that is what I would call bad behavior on their part, although I am not saying that this happens intentionally.

Let me explain that the profits they gain for these medications are a lot more than they would pay in any lawsuit, which is partly why they are willing to take the risk of having someone die from any one medication. The United States is known to have spent $238.4 billion on health care a year, according to Statista.com. There are more lobbyists in Washington and more lawyers than anyone can imagine. They give benefits to hospitals and doctors who will prescribe the medications they suggest all the way down to you. Also, it seems that the American public has a short memory or a nonexistent one when they hear about a pharmaceutical company being sued for a loss of life from a medication. There has rarely been any talk of boycotting a pharmaceutical company for this bad behavior. It seems like a frequent occurrence. Maybe when this oversight does occur, they keep any unfavorable news from reaching the public. We must stop this unconscionable lack of regard for humanity. We must make ourselves better educated and stop believing everything the pharmaceutical companies tell us. Let me explain that the pharmaceutical companies are making a killing quite literally here. I guess the real question here is could we do better for ourselves? Or could lives be saved?

A

WHO WANTS TO PLAY RUSSIAN ROULETTE WITH THEIR HEALTH?

The so-called system doesn't work for everyone. Many people are being left behind, to put it bluntly.

You must ask yourself if there is a dollar sign on your health, and the answer is you bet there is. It's well known that doctors make mistakes every year due to human error, and there are illnesses that we have no known cures for. For the illnesses that we do have cures for, I'm only asking why they decided to make all these medicines that don't work and only some that do what we expect them to. What choice would you make for yourself or your family if you had the knowledge or were informed of the medications that work and the ones that don't?

Where did we go wrong? And the answer, unfortunately, is greed. We must ask ourselves if the pharmaceutical companies are benevolent to our needs or if they are only concerned with the perpetuation and dominance of their own. For many of us this is uncharted territory.

It's very easy to find out which medications treat which illnesses. Unfortunately, we are being blitzed with ads by the pharmaceutical companies to treat every possible illness that we think we have, and a lot of them we have never heard of before. I don't know about you, but I certainly don't trust any of these ads with all the caveats that are attached to them. Most times, it seems like the side effects are worse than having the illness. We have a history in our country of putting people on some of the older medications that don't work as well as others and leaving them there.

We have had a turn of events in this country with people losing all regard for life and, most unfortunately to me, innocent people losing their lives. With a great number of people not being on the road to recovery for their mental illness, we are in a dire situation. I'm not here to talk about your amendment rights, but the bottom line is most of our country has been denied the one most personal and given right to their lives, to be well, through the dysfunction of our health-care system. Our health-care system has not been serving us and is deemed "too big to fail," which not only undermines the health of one person but puts most of the entire country at risk.

Why are people suffering from mental illness when we have the science to help them live functional lives? Doesn't anyone ever look at the economic and financial loss of one community to the rest of the country? Even though I am without symptoms at this point and consider this the best time in my life, I can't just turn my back and leave all the other people behind when I know they are suffering.

Along my journey to recovery, I met hundreds of people in their forties or fifties still searching after twenty years for the right doctor to treat them with the right combination of medicines, even thinking that electric shock therapy would help, which it only does in a small percentage of the population. I've met people in their seventies with depression who have suffered for over fifty years and have been on every medication that was out there. Wouldn't we all want to be treated better than this? It seems like we have to take risks with our health. Trust is the most beneficial trait in the marketplace for good health, and where you get your information from matters. Don't give away your most important asset without a fight.

ASSETS OF THE HEALTH-CARE SYSTEM

According to the *Commonwealth Fund Report*, the United States is dead last regarding quality of care, access, or equity of healthy lives in comparison to other large countries. Because America has the stance that we should capitalize on the health-care system, we give up a universal health-care system and the benefits that come with it, such as quality and access to care.

This has resulted in the lessening of good health care throughout our country. At the very least, what we can rely on through the federal health department is being alerted if there is an epidemic like the coronavirus, a virus that has taken too many good people from us, and diseases like HIV that used to take our lives. In different packages, these diseases seem to appear more and more. I would hope that most people are aware of how badly the government's reaction was when the first cases of HIV appeared in our gay population. This is another example of stigma operating against a certain portion of our people who were blamed and punished for being who they were.

Originally, when HIV first appeared, people got a second test six months later for confirmation to know that the first test was correct. Before this time, it was not looked upon as a mistake if needles were used twice in hospitals. I am pleased to say that in the last three decades, HIV research has continued to the point where most people are able to tolerate the medications and live relatively normal lives.

After the health-care system, you have the support of your family, groups that may advocate for you, or your social worker and doctors. If you do not listen to them or are not able to negotiate for the best medical treatment available, you very much may end up in a hospital if diagnosed with mental illness.

When you are in a hospital, if you are not a danger to yourself or society, it will be up to a judge who will generally decide to release you. Because of the expenditure of hundreds of billions of dollars a year on the health-care system for mental illness—it is minimally up to sixty thousand dollars a year to institutionalize one person—the system is corrupted by greed. The pharmaceutical industry is also cleaning up. If you are in the system and are getting what you deem to be the best medication and you can negotiate with your doctor to work for your benefit rather than the industry's, your chances of getting better improve. You can also call the FDA to ask about information on current medications that are being considered for distribution in the marketplace.

Nonetheless, professionals in the health-care system generally don't tell you about nutrition, diet, exercise, and the endless homework to get healthy. This is where it's good to have an advocate you trust to negotiate for you. Do your own research as well. This is why I am writing this book. It's also necessary to know what is available to you in all medical fields.

I believe it should be known that there are only 46,000 psychiatrists to serve about 51.9 million people with a diagnosis, and the responsibilities are falling to our family doctors. This may make it harder to get the right medicine, or even a diagnosis. I have always felt people are getting less consideration, and I hope that changes for the better.

PROBLEMS AND SOLUTIONS AND THE BREAKING POINT

Some problems loosely related to behavior are psychological. Sometimes these problems seem unresolvable by accessible knowledge; these include behaviors that are antisocial, destructive, or disruptive in a broad sense. The process of finding solutions to neurological afflictions is not always successful because they have to do with neural processors and aberrations in the brain. A sense of responsibility is always a good response, yet the human function of a person is not always based on manners. If you have a diagnosis, it could take years of caring and understanding to get the functional brain to process again. The goal is to have a good set of values and morals toward others and a cognitive way of thinking.

For the caregiver, it takes years of commitment to the person's well-being to have a future for someone with a diagnosis. It also takes empathy and patience over a long time. Reverse psychology, the power of suggestion, and problem-solution exercises can help. A sense of learning leads to a sense of conformity in society.

If someone has a break with reality, the breaking point could be at any time of extreme stress or anxiety. Transition is a hard time to achieve things, like graduating school, and basic things like taking care of yourself can seem overwhelming. When violence or trauma takes over a life, like in the battlefields with improvised explosive devices (IEDs) or shell shock, these sets of circumstances, with the lack of humanity in the world, can create a break from normal reality in the mind. Hopefully, these people will be rectified by therapy, health care, and a healthier lifestyle. Let's build on our reach for the well-being of our military and families. We all need a support system.

THE HUMAN TOLL AND
THE DIAGNOSTIC

In numbers, the number of people with depression is extreme, and that has no sign of changing anytime in the future. The recovery rate for schizophrenia is 14.35% over 10 years and for depression 41 percent over a lifetime, considering that mild to moderate cases are more recoverable than extreme cases, but keep in mind that some medications do not work as well as others, which leads me to believe that the recovery rate for depression may be incorrect. The human toll for our families, friends, and neighbors across the country is massive, and we are all paying the real price for these illnesses. Unfortunately, a health industry based on profit rather than your recovery puts the odds of getting well against you. In a wealthy country like ours, we take having the necessities of life for granted, but, sadly, there is no way to replace good health and a reasonable quality of life. There is only so much time on this earth for all of us.

People are diagnosed because mental illness is defined by three precursors: drugs, trauma, and genetics. Because there is nothing that we can really do with genetics at this time, which I brought up in my circumstances earlier in this book, because it exists in every family tree, we focus on the other two. Determining what the exact cause is may be, like looking for a needle in a haystack. The condition that a person has may be passed down from five generations in their genetic code. The environment where your forefathers lived may be important to some of these diagnoses. For example, with bipolar depression, it is known that it is more prevalent in people of Ashkenazi or Eastern European descent. Also, illicit drugs of any kind can play a role in getting a mental illness diagnosis, and trauma can cause a break from reality as well.

A

FINDING THE RIGHT DOCTOR

I've always believed that going to a specialist is better than going to a family doctor or someone just fluent with psychiatry. There are great doctors out there who will put their life on the line for you every day. There are also doctors who create a hypocrisy and let the industry define their actions rather than preserve the human condition. Unfortunately, when you are dealing with a psychiatrist, there are a lot of doctors who mainly practice cognitive therapy. There are some doctors who are very good at being able to make a diagnosis. There are also many doctors who are interested in finding the right medication that will give you your life back. There is also a chapter about the percentages of people who get the help they need with the medication that they deserve.

I once had a doctor who treated me who was about to lose her own life. She saved my life but unfortunately couldn't save her own because she was suffering from an incurable heart condition. She had the most compassion that I ever encountered in the medical system. In most of my experiences, my psychiatrists, in general, just whitewashed over my symptoms and tried to show that they had the license and authority to get me to accept whatever medication or therapy that they were pushing. And so begins this game of pacifying patients versus the industries' cost of saving lives, like the victim and the bad guy in relationships. In a lot of cases, these lifesaving strokes of justice are performed in times of regard to humanity against the opposite of indifference. This dichotomy unfortunately results in a lot of people feeling that they have not been well served by their doctors. And the truth is some haven't been. It is very rare that the first medication that is prescribed for someone will work the best for him or her. Most medications take time to be effective, and some do not work as well for any given individual.

The other thing that is never discussed is that a doctor wants to know that he or she is treating someone who wants to get well for him or her to put in the time to find the right medication. Most of them are not interested in treating someone who wants to throw his or her life away. This is something that should concern you and something that should make you change every habit in your life, considering that you do want your life back. After you're initially diagnosed, you want to find a doctor who is experienced with your condition and knows the current medications that will give you the best impact on your health.

PROS AND CONS IN THIS INDUSTRY

There are pros and cons in this industry, especially when looking to get treated or trying to get a friend or family member treated. If you have an enormous amount of money, you can go to a private clinic for $10,000 to $12,000 a week until you're well. Once again, we find that money talks. I always say that the best pros are always the best cons. If you're looking for a prospective doctor to treat you with the one medication that works for you, you might do better going to a hospital rather than a private psychiatrist. This is because, frequently, private psychiatrists will treat you with the medication of their choice rather than the one that works unless you specifically request otherwise. Usually, a person with trauma is in a state of shock, and the first doctor that you choose for any analysis or therapy can make a difference for the rest of your life.

You want to make sure that the psychiatrist that you see is knowledgeable about new medications and the updated research on chemistry. When you're starting a search for your first doctor, they generally will tell you whether they work with one specific diagnosis. Also, you should consider talking to your doctor about getting off any unnecessary medications because these will slow or prevent your recovery. If you see only one psychiatrist at the onset who prescribes the wrong medication, you may be stuck for a lifetime if your search ends there. If the medication you're prescribed doesn't help with your symptoms or the side effects are too severe, you would want to share this information with your doctor so specific changes can be made.

You don't want to use a psychotropic medication that doesn't even work but can lead to your getting another illness entirely. This is hardly a fair trade. Also, private psychiatrists may always prescribe the medication they believe in, but they don't always have the facility to accommodate a person with a specific illness through hospitalization. There are only certain medications that some psychiatrists can prescribe because of the limitations on their access. You may be treated with a drug that was sent to some doctor as a sample to make a profit if he or she prescribed that one medication. In fact, most people who are treated one time by a private psychiatrist are given a medication that doesn't seem to work or works only as a startup medication. Again, it's trial and error to get the medications that work best. This could leave the patient with a lifetime of symptoms never treated and a lifetime of cruelty that leads to an untimely, uneasy demise. I call this, at the least, less than merciful. Let's try to serve our consumers better than that.

GETTING INFORMATION

When you do get a diagnosis after a traumatic episode, getting information about your specific condition can be a longtime endeavor. When you go to a psychiatric facility, they will give you general information about your condition and what medications they are willing to prescribe. The more you're truthful and outright about your symptoms, the better chance a doctor will be able to treat you with the right medication.

Although you may be offered cognitive therapy, if you have severe cell and neurological damage to the brain, you're not going to get the recovery that you're looking for right away, and it certainly isn't going to happen overnight. If you've been on several medications and don't feel that they've been effective, this may make going to a hospital your better choice. And we all know that in the hospital cafeteria, doctors talk about the medications that work and the ones that don't. Based on my personal experience, Clozaril is the best medicine on the market for schizophrenia and depression, and that's what all the psychiatrists have told me, but doctors are reluctant to prescribe it because you must have a blood draw every month to confirm that it is not affecting your white blood cell count. And necessarily, it is only prescribed as the third medicine to help with the recovery of schizophrenia. I feel very lucky that this medication worked for me, especially when I see people in their seventies who are still suffering from not being given the right medication. This is a lifetime of illness that is unnecessary in my view. Other than this one drawback, this medication works 99 percent of the time throughout a lifetime.

Seeing many doctors in a hospital setting will give you the advantage of getting many opinions, and even then, you may find that you must negotiate to get this medication prescribed for you. Usually, they will only prescribe Clozaril after two other medications have been tried and found not to work. It took me thirteen years before they finally prescribed it for me, and I started on my road to recovery. I do believe that hospitals have more useful tools at hand to treat you and will give you better, more up-to-date information and diagnostics to get you on the road to recovery. I can't emphasize enough that being informed about your illness puts the odds in your favor, rather than you becoming the victim of others playing roulette with your health.

Be aware that some negative things can happen in a hospital as well. During one of my hospitalizations, I was denied a nicotine patch for no apparent reason. This certainly didn't help me cope with recovering from the psychosis that had brought me in there. Also, the doctor who was treating me discriminated against the people I was living with and my family, saying that there was cocaine found in my bloodstream, which was not true. He seemed to think that this would limit places that I could go to so that he could refer me to an institution of his choice. Of course, he was going to receive payment for doing the paperwork to do this. Looking back, I feel now that his reasons were unjustifiable and that his motives were entirely about his financial gain. Since we must acknowledge that the state can take away your freedoms, having representation or advocacy when you're in the hospital can help you a great deal.

This is a corrupt mental health-care system that we live with, and you need to acknowledge this to move through it. It doesn't mean that all doctors are corrupt, but there are problems with a lot of the institutions that we must deal with. When you do not have representation or advocacy on your side, you can expect a certain amount of neglect or discrimination, which can cost years of your life. This neglect should in no way give you any reason to stop living your life but should raise an awareness of the kinds of problems that you will encounter on your road to recovery. If you stay positive and play by the rules, you will find that hospitalization can be a new start to finding the help you need for your future.

HOW TO GET ON THE RIGHT MEDICATIONS

Remember each aspect of this book has necessary parts, such as troubleshooting. The real problem with having to deal with a psychiatrist and getting on the right medication is how long the duration is between your diagnosis and getting the treatment that you know works. I've already stated that I believe Clozaril is the best medication for schizophrenia and depression. You do have to know that there is a science to recovery that is available, and you must work with your doctor to find the best medical treatment plan for you. When I first started on Clozaril in 2000, I was started on a very high dose, but after that, every year, the dosage went down as the symptoms started to disappear. After six and a half years, the symptoms were minimal, and I had planned to recover by the time I was forty-five. Another five years later, with the help of nutrition and analysis, I was doing well.

This medicine works ninety-nine out of a hundred times, if you can tolerate it from the beginning. Every medication has side effects, but, fortunately for me, the worst side effect was sleeping a lot. Nonetheless, if I asked you if you would take ten medications over a lifetime that basically didn't work or take one that works to the extent of controlling all your symptoms and giving you back your life, I think you would answer in favor of the second. It's really a question that shouldn't have to be asked. When you are put on Clozaril, the medical requirement is that you've already tried at least two medications that didn't work. Because the right information was not available to me for eleven years of my illness, I felt that the time that I spent was unnecessary because I was uninformed. You should do your own private search to find out what medications are given for your specific condition. (Look at the chapter about doing your homework.) This is one of the most important questions you will have to answer.

A

ARE WE AT THE MERCY OF THE SYSTEM?

If you or a family member gets a diagnosis, you may feel blindsided or alone. Medicine is based on hypothesis and may not work for everyone. There is no perfect science. And the so-called system doesn't work for everyone. You may feel underserved as a consumer. It could happen to anyone in any situation. This does not justify the idea of stigma, which is to alienate a person and his or her ideals and values and put him or her further away from recovery. Stigma is part of our culture but should not be part of the psychiatric system that we depend upon in our society. What the industry does provide is medical benefits, psychiatric care, and other clinical help, such as sociology or analysis. What you do have to know when you are put on medication is that not all medications work the same, and some have been pulled off the shelf because of their side effects. There are also institutions that can help you with housing and getting necessities, such as food stamps. Although these services are often difficult to attain, you should persevere if you feel you are entitled to them.

The best thing that you can do is to stay on a plan, educate yourself about your condition, and get the best professional care that you can find. A working chemistry between you and a doctor or therapist is also essential to find. This relationship between you and a therapist should be considered sacred. Getting closure on past relationships and unresolved issues will help you to get answers to your current questions and bring you back to the present time. If you are hospitalized and don't have a place to live, doctors can benefit you by putting you in small institutes. This is not based on getting you the best psychiatric care, but hopefully you will be able to use the resources available to you to get on the right track toward recovery and a good living situation. (See the chapter about "Troubleshooting" if you're in a situation where you feel that your health and well-being are in some danger.) There are legal constructs available to you if you feel that you need an advocate, such as the department of the mentally ill and NAMI (the National Association for the Mentally Ill).We may also want to say that this is the best system we have got if it was a perfect world. I feel that it is, unfortunately, not a perfect world. At best, the sense of consciousness bound by the consumer in any state of resolve or for stability or necessity to have a treatment plan that includes a recovery plan for a curable affliction and a moral obligation rather than based on luck or chance, anything less would be an attempt to argue the state of disability, such as mental illness, is less than empathetic or remorseful, which I don't believe it is. And that said, without basic trust, there is the possibility that the system would break down itself entirely. In reality, it's almost impossible to attain any type of guarantee.

NOSTALGIA AND THE MEDIA

What we see in the media in general is that there is new cognitive therapy available to treat some types of mental illness. However, stigma becomes a firestorm when some mentally ill person commits a violent crime and temporarily brings our lack of treatment of the mentally ill to the forefront. This country has seen way too many incidents where a person with a mental diagnosis is blamed for a strange or horrific event. Unfortunately, there are always bad apples in the barrel, whether people have a diagnosable condition or not. The chances that a person will have an undiagnosed mental illness are comparable to the massive number of people being treated with the wrong medication, and we are bearing the pain of our personal losses because of it. The percentage of people with a mental diagnosis, which is approximately one-fifth of the population, commit fewer crimes than the other four-fifths without a diagnosis. To say that the mentally ill in this country are not discriminated against is a blatant lie. We have a long, shameful history of incarcerating vulnerable, defenseless people and not giving them treatment during their incarceration. This was entirely prevalent until very recently, and even now the medications that are given may not be the ones that can give them any kind of recovery. Unfortunately, we have a huge society that would rather profit by these illnesses than treat them. This puts the chances of recovery against you. It is my sincerest hope that with a new awareness of the huge numbers of our population who are suffering from this stigma, we can change lives and create a more benevolent society.

A

STEPS FOR PTSD
AND THE VETERANS
ADMINISTRATION WITH THE
METAPHOR OF CARDS

M any veterans return from overseas with PTSD, which used to be called shell shock. Although veterans returning from battle have a learning curve as to redefining how to live in a civil society, I believe that the Veterans Administration (VA) can best support them in this endeavor. It's unfortunate that some of these conditions are ingrained into our veterans because of the service that they were asked to perform. When anyone asks people to put their lives on the line for a cause, there should be a good reason. And any veteran deserves to know that his or her service is valued. No war has been fought and has gone as planned, yet the political system has changed many times in our history, and that does affect the reasons that people have been in the service. Whatever war someone served in, the social phobias can continue to this day even if the war was generations ago. This also means that there are reasons for mistrust and denial for veterans. Having said that, I think that the VA is still the best program available to help veterans get over the problems that are or have been evident in the recovery of any condition that they face.

Even with the social phobias that exist, educating yourself about your illness is valid and will help define the type of health care that you receive. I believe that the VA provides the best health care for our veterans, whether they served overseas or at home.

If you have a deck of cards and the nine of clubs symbolizes the trauma that you have experienced in your life, anytime that you see that same card, the nine of clubs, it brings up the experience of that trauma. Nonetheless, if you are able to get analysis and be specific about the incident and the trauma that you have faced, when you see the nine of clubs, that experience loses its significance in your life, the incident is less valid and relevant to deal with. If all of the cards in the deck were all the nine of clubs, which we know not to be true, all you would think about would be that specific incident. Seeing the nine of clubs, we know that there is only one nine of clubs in a deck of cards, thereby lessening the idea of trauma and anxiety that exists.

EDUCATION AND STEPS TO TAKE TOWARD RECOVERY

And Confidence and Wisdom

What has been documented is that the medication that is used for mild to moderate depression does not always work for severe depression, which is defined as a person who has up to four major depressive episodes in one year. For this severe category, the medication is said to just be helpful. The same is said for schizophrenia, except ten out of twelve medications didn't work for me over a lifetime. What you must do is your own personal research by talking to doctors and people who have recovered from your illness and find out what worked for them. I know that it's hard to envision a lifetime of medication ahead of you when you first get diagnosed, but if you don't accept this, you will be hindering the possibility of your recovery along the way. You should also be clear about the type of side effects from the medication that you and your doctor decide to go along with.

These two concepts may be the most important in the long run. Just like the idea of knowledge being power, confidence in yourself and wisdom learned from experience can create an effect on the direction that your life is going. The better the judgment that you have, the better the decisions that you make, which directly affects the consequences that you face in the future. Confidence is not only a belief in yourself but a belief in the decisions that you make and how you deal with them. Wisdom and experience can help you to create or define your character and the dreams of a future for yourself. Applying wisdom can help you to have the destiny that you want. And if, or when, you put yourself in this position, the world can be your oyster. Remember every day is a new day to make your dreams come true.

TRANSITIONING BACK AND WORKING FOR THE FUTURE

L ooking back with hindsight is always easier than trying to predict the future. After all, you gain knowledge and experience as you proceed in life, and that knowledge and experience helps to make you better at knowing the future. It gives you the benefit of filling in answers to questions that you may have. What circumstances you may have in the future cannot always be predicted so consider that there is an element of mystery in looking at the future and especially in the idea of recovery.

Almost always the best thing that you can do is use whatever knowledge you have. I recently have been getting my best information on the internet and from professionals I know. If you want to get the best information for your future, be sure to learn from your mistakes, which means listening to professionals and asking questions. This means doing your homework and putting your best foot forward. That's what I did, and it led to writing this book. Consider getting a better education and work experience that can benefit you in the long run when you're looking at your life ten or twenty years later. This can give you a great deal of gratification knowing that you have accomplished something with your life. These decisions should be made after you're under treatment with professional care and have whatever benefits are available to you. You should know after your initial diagnosis, you can then apply for Supplemental Security Income (SSI), Social Security Disability (SSD), Supplemental Nutrition Assistance Program (SNAP) benefits, help with heating and electricity, and so on.

It's hard when you get a diagnosis at whatever age to know what circumstances you are facing or how hard it may be to deal with the onset of mental illness. Changing the situation may be the first thing you should do, along with getting the best professional care. Although you may or may not be told about your recovery when you are first diagnosed, the time that you spend does not have to be worthless. Listening to your doctor and having a plan is the start to recovery. There are several things you can do to start recovery. Here are a few basic ideas that are good to know.

1. Taking care of yourself must be first.
2. Respecting boundaries is a mutual concept.
3. Have a medical plan with your doctor or therapist.
4. Be a person with pride in having control over the abstract objects in your life.
5. Benefit yourself by participating in whatever group activities you can and gaining the social regard of other people who may be in the same situation as you.
6. Understand that being positive may be the best way to create a bridge between you and other people.
7. Taking care of your material things and having pride in those things you own shows you have respect for yourself and those around you.

PERSEVERANCE PAYS OFF AND THE LIGHT AT THE END OF THE TUNNEL

I f you continually look for the good in life, you will see whatever is there. If you pursue being able to change what is there, you make the first step in changing the world. Always know you have something to give back. In our human condition, there are always so many people looking for help, you can become very popular by providing whatever is needed to help others and profit by it. If I had given up when I had been given my first medication, I would have lived with a lifetime of disability. Persevering to find the right answers that will help you the most will save you a lot of time and energy down the line.

There is always a diamond in the rough out there. Many people will walk right by you and not notice you, and a few others will see something special in you and want to invest no matter what shape you're in. If you truly invest in yourself and are true to your soul, you will find others who are also unique, and you can join your path with theirs. Do not be the one who leaves that diamond on the ground. Find people you have things in common with and invest in the kind of lifestyle that you want to be in, no matter what your situation is now.

After being in the mental health-care system for twenty-eight years, I realized that I had a diagnosis that only 14.35 percent can recover from. I made a pledge to educate people so that they would be able to find their way to the same place in recovery that I had gotten to. This involved creating a map to show people the exact way to navigate the system and create a safe place for themselves with the hope that no one would be left behind. I believe that everyone deserves good care and that the future of the science of mental illness will include being able to offer many choices for recovery. This might include surgery as well as giving the right medications at the onset of psychosis. I hope that people can gain the quality of life included with socialization and proper medical care within a system that works for all individuals.

TROUBLESHOOTING AND DECISION-MAKING

There may come a time when a person is under too much stress or his or her condition is overlooked to the point that that person may need to be observed or be hospitalized. The two benefits out of this situation are that this person will be observed by professionals, and it will lay out a time to assess the treatment and the chemistry of that person and, if needed, change his or her medications. It may take time to go through this process, but in some cases, this might be an incredible opportunity. This is a good time to suggest a new regimen. This is the time when a doctor may make decisions about your health. I was hospitalized for the ninth time in Beth Israel Hospital in New York City and was there for four months. The best thing that came out of that was that they finally gave me the best drug for schizophrenia, clozapine, which was the drug that saved my life. The only two things that were difficult in a city hospital were that I was claustrophobic and tried to deal with it in the best way that I could.

We make decisions all the time, and we judge ourselves even more. We might make small decisions about what clothes to wear in the morning, yet we make harder decisions about how to save a life. In my view, this is just as important as serving your country. If we were all able to save just one life, consider how much better a life we could have for all of us. The harder decision of the act of saving a life is not something that you think about though. It's a human apparatus. We are not always successful, but it is better than never trying. The lesson to learn is to not give up.

IMPORTANCE OF RECOVERY

No matter how much morality and intelligence I can put into this book, it does come down to the sum of its parts and how effectively they are used. The goal is obviously to help others recover. I could just say this out of common decency, but I would not be writing this book unless I believed that some of these illnesses are curable, and people can have a better quality of life.

If I get caught up in the disarray of my life, I practice counting the nine of clubs (see the chapter "Steps for PTSD and the Veterans Administration with the Metaphor of Cards") until I recognize the point at which I felt traumatized so that I will know exactly what to tell my therapist when I go to talk to him or her. Years and years ago, I realized that I would forget what I wanted to tell my therapist so I would write a list of those things that bothered me to be able to convey it to him or her. Putting that list on paper is extremely important so that I can move on and be more effective. This makes me know that I have a team with my psychiatrist and therapist as a contractual agreement to move on with my health.

Personally, I collected twelve years of information before writing this book so that you don't have to. I also made a recovery date and achieved that date of recovery. Sometimes, all that perseverance doesn't help. In that case, when you look back at your achievements, they may seem trivial, but the goal of recovery is the ultimate gift that you could ask for from anyone. Recovery is as significant as seeing that double rainbow.

This isn't just about life; it is about the justification that we all want to say, "Nothing is going to stop me." The satisfaction of our very existence is in our hands and those of the people we depend upon. We can change our condition together. So, when you look back, look hard, and look twice. Recovery means being informed, educated, and ready to challenge yourself to be the best possible person you can be.

A POSITIVE ATTITUDE AND ROLE-PLAYING

t's been said that having a positive attitude determines your direction. I believe it determines a lot more than that. If you have a positive attitude, good things tend to come your way. If you remove yourself from the outcome of situations, you have a much better chance of not being disappointed. Some people are more skeptical than others about their lives, but no matter what you believe in, good things happen to even the unluckiest of people. So, keep your head up because you may have your day in the park as well. If you have good intentions going into any circumstances, you've already profited from the situation if you don't expect anything back. Knowing that you are going to benefit from any situation is the best way to listen and get new information. People respond to others who have a positive attitude, and you'll find that doctors and professionals are much happier to share their knowledge with you because of this.

Role-playing is an interesting dynamic. The definition of role-playing, according to the *Dictionary of Psychology* is "the acting out in an appropriate fashion of the role one perceives as properly characteristic of oneself and is widely used in psychotherapy or education." It takes several people with the same type of problem and allows them to experience what others would do in the same situation. So, if you're sitting in a circle in a room, as the discussion goes around the room, you tend to get deeper into regular life situations. There is always one bad apple in the batch, yet that person is usually the one who's more ignored. As a therapy group, you will find out more and more about each other, so you get the answers from the questions that you would want to be asked yourself. As you do this, you find out the similarities between people. This paradox is not just communication; it's also a chance to get therapy and find out that you're no different than anyone else. Then outside that group you can create a porthole and show others that the individual in you is stronger than just a group but better than alone. It's the best of all possible worlds.

The last metaphor I can give you is that if you're making a wave in a stadium each time your team scores, I think that you would be able to learn any game that was played. And playing that game is to help everyone know you're playing on a team. Consider a group like that or even better. You can usually locate a therapy group in your area that concentrates on your diagnosis. You're not playing in this arena alone. We're all on the same team.

A

SOCIAL AGREEMENTS

This includes regular doctors, therapists, psychiatrists, or even your mom if you are so lucky to be blessed. Professionals have a moral obligation to do whatever is needed to help you. This is a great thing. It's better that we have these relationships than just the personal ones. We all know those types of social contracts that someone can break anytime that he or she chooses. There are also social contracts that, suddenly, become obligations and are just not fun anymore. I lived in a communal house where there was no autonomy or basic freedoms, and it made it very difficult for me to access my basic needs. Once I realized that I was in the wrong place for me to try to recover, I used all my resources to find a better situation for myself. However, the simplicity of a personal contract can be useful in other ways.

I think that all of us are essentially looking for a caregiver. It's certainly a nice feeling to know that someone has your back in this sometimes-difficult world. As life changes over time, though, there are relationships that we tend to cut loose for whatever reason. Surviving the breakup of an intimate relationship can make us stronger in the long run.

Can you imagine a world where most people will have a mental or physical diagnosis in their lifetime? This is the world that we live in now, yet we separate ourselves by stigmatizing another who has a different diagnosis than we do. We should stop calling ourselves humanity if we don't practice being humane. Are we judging the progress of our world on creating new technology that might take us to Mars one day or how many people are still the subjects of genocide and are starving through no fault of their own? When will most of the people learn that everyone on our planet is interconnected? It is through consciousness that we exist and through consciousness that we will die.

When groups of people come together in a common cause, we are made aware of the fact that our commonality outweighs our differences. A world where everyone has a better day than the previous one shows the true progress that we are making on this planet. Try looking in the mirror and asking yourself if your reflection is different than someone else's or if your reflection is closer to the same. Why are we spending so much time and energy focused on the differences between us when all we must do is extend the same respect and regard for others that we hold for ourselves? If you can step back and acknowledge that your opinions and subsequent actions were formed from all the past experiences in your life, it might help you to have more compassion for others. Try applying the "walk a mile in my shoes" adage before you show disrespect for another's opinion.

A

FINDING SUCCESS

I f I could wave my magic wand and make everything in your life healthy and proper, I would love to do that. Unfortunately, the way the story goes is that you build your life and your foundation one day at a time, and day by day, you get closer to the health and goals that you want. Nothing comes easy in this world, but it does get better, and once you start taking care of yourself, your nutrition, and your environment, you will see that this world takes notice of your efforts. And the better you feel about yourself, the better you are perceived by others—even if it's just one day after the next.

Once you do your homework and attain this knowledge to recover, you become one of those people who can be empowered. The trick is to get noticed by people at the top or philanthropists who want a person like you to get an education, work for a Fortune 500 company, or just achieve some of your personal goals. Don't be shy about calling people that you know, taking risks, and seeing if they have a position that might be available to you. Even if you're working part-time or at a base level, there may be positions higher up that you would qualify for. You might be amazed that some people are open to hiring people with disabilities. The higher you go up that ladder, the closer you get to attaining your dreams.

You will see it's been right with you the whole time. What's amazing to me is that as we get closer to our dreams, we realize that it's been in us the whole time. We ourselves are the most amazing creatures in the world; no matter how difficult life might seem, we so hope to better our lost potential. Whether it's looking through rose-colored glasses or not, put yourself in a long-term goal of achieving success, happiness, and evolution, even if it starts with staying in bed for an extra hour in the morning just to get your energy up. Isn't this better than feeling like you just can't seem to reach that brass ring? Make it. Consider pursuing your dreams.

WHAT IT IS LIKE TO BE MENTALLY ILL AND VISIONS FOR THE FUTURE

I t is said that people who are mentally ill are compromised. This is a hard topic to deal with, and it gets a bad rap. It is said that a diagnosis affects your survival. It is a complex situation to deal with. The statement that someone is approving of your state of mind is extremely important.

Then you may be able to prove that the state of mind you are in is not compromised.

This may be the worst pain that does not go away. In terms of resolve, you must cherish these moments, because you're not alone in wanting a perfect life. These agreements are based on your well-being. If you are not able to pay for medicine and advice, there are reasons to supplement these monetary values. It should not be considered fluff. It is important. You know that pushing forward is really the only way to overcome the cruelty you may be experiencing. The feeling that there is no way to be in control of your health is a terrible feeling to live with. Remember that your health is in your hands ultimately, and there is kindness in the world. In terms of mental health, these issues that you deal with, and the connotation of the words *mental illness* are not written in granite.

Despite the word *illness*, you may still be able to obtain health and be considered a person who is functioning at a high level. You can be well adjusted, rather than ill in some fashion or meaning. In one way or another, we all continue to be able to process our thoughts and emotions. How we do this is not just a choice; it is a function of who we are. It does not necessarily go away, but in some cases, it does get better. Getting the knowledge to resolve issues can be a necessary goal.

PERCEPTION AND SOCIAL CONTRACTS

When you make an agreement, such as with your psychiatrist and social worker, it is your responsibility to keep that agreement, knowing that it is about your well-being. Is this how we create reciprocity? Remember that you are not building Rome in one day. If you feel that the rules do not work for you, then you must negotiate change. The good points of your life are the ones that matter—pushing forward is the only way to recover from the cruelty that you are dealing with. Remember that your health is in your hands, ultimately, and there is kindness in the world. The silent pandemic is no longer silent.

As a vision for the future, I hope that science and medicine continue to evolve. I hope that with the aid of better nutrition, better care, and the loss of stigma in our society, we can all lead better and more fulfilling lives. I look forward to a day when all of our symptoms are treated, and research continues to move forward. I see us being the best of ourselves intertwined with respect and regard for all people, races, sexes, and creeds. This includes the interest of better research and quality of life for all.

According to my own perception, I really wasn't supposed to be healthy, because in my mind, God had made me this way. Knowing that I had issues that I considered to be reality or just entertainment, I, in fact, just wanted to make everything nicer for the next person in my life. I moved into my mother's house in 2019 and became very close to her. She tried to teach me about taking care of a home and being a mensch. Knowing people and gaining personal knowledge has had a huge impact on my perception of myself. I spent a lot of time on this subject because there was always something new to fix. I have always felt that giving back when you don't expect something in return is the way to benefit yourself the most.

After a certain amount of time, I finally got my mother to make a schedule for me so that we could be on the same page, and of course, if it's not broken, don't fix it. I realized that she was doing 60 percent care rather than my 40 percent. But no one is counting, which had a direct cause and effect on the social rules that we played by. I felt like I was on a mission to better myself. I felt like the bond between us helped me to be a better person. In truth, real experiences are the best models for your perception. When we gain knowledge from our personal experiences, we are the benefactors. It helps define our own personal strengths and our perception of ourselves and the world.

Mental illness can affect your survival in all ways. This is not compromised. The reason that you must care is that you have someone who feels loss and whom you can believe in. Mental illness does not.

COMMUNICATION AND RECOVERY MYTHS

Everything is based on the concept of communication. The more clearly you communicate, the more likely you are to get what you want—that's the bottom line. Whom you communicate to and how you resolve any matter that may come up is your responsibility. Be fair to whomever you have agreements with. That can pay off. Communication is a basis to all the answers that you endeavor to know. How you play your cards on the table of life can be an experiment. Consider making a list of the things that you want, and profit from that investment. We all have core functions to be able to get the things that we desire. A relationship with another person can lead very easily into denial. There's something in social psychology called a comparison level. This means that people have expectations of each other in a relationship. There is an average overall level of personal interaction and expectation between individuals. People with high comparison levels expect to have rewarding and fulfilling relationships with others. If you have a lower comparison, it leads you to be less committed to a relationship and becomes a catch-22.

Communication can be the key to be able to negotiate to further improve the quality of your life and be able to fulfill your needs.

If you're hurting, acknowledge that you're hurting, get the help that you need, and understand that you need to take care of your survival first. Consider that the answers are here at your feet. The way that you're able to communicate will define your ability to recover. Stand up, and let your voice be heard. You have nothing to lose.

We all have our own point of view. It's not a crime to be alone or be hurting. We don't live on a desert island. No one survives alone in this world. Try to find the confidence that you need to express yourself. There may be times when you may need to find whatever leverage or social power that you can. Build on whatever skills you have and remember that things start and end with communication.

Here I am outlining some of my basic philosophy about all the things that I have written about in this book.

1. I do not advocate the use of electroshock therapy.

2. I do believe that everyone can recover or, if treated right, can get to a better place, even if people say that because of the person's diagnosis, he or she cannot recover.

3. Pushing people like cattle into institutions was a poor way to treat problems we may have, but letting the mentally ill go homeless or be untreated in jails is not any better.

4. Isolation is perhaps the worst thing you can do to someone. It can cause trauma that will last a lifetime.

5. If you don't include vitamins and minerals, such as in fish oil and so on, and pay attention to the health

side of your life, even though you are taking your prescribed medications, you are cutting down your recovery rate by 40 percent.

6. Make it very clear to anyone on your case if you have allergies because those allergies can affect you very seriously.

7. Always have a plan to be able to troubleshoot a situation if you must be in the hospital even for a short amount of time.

8. Know that there is a set pattern that shows that certain treatments work and understand which ones don't.

All people, at some time in their lives, go down the rabbit hole. So rather than believing that there's a perfect reality, which we know is not true, I justified this by trying to rationalize my thinking, although in my chronic state, I may have little or no understanding of my state of consciousness or mental health and the better I'm informed the more well off I am. I have felt my sense of reality, had been broken, psychologically and socially. So metaphorically speaking, there was a split in the road of life in a way and I felt I had to choose a direction to go in. In truth, what I had to do was remove myself from the situation that I was in and the equation itself entirely and make sense of what was, the best positive direction to take in my life, rather than any sort of drama.

Step 2 in this scenario I must realize that everything could be relative, and a simple set of labels could help me in setting a direction to go in. It turns out that fixing those things that are broken is not so easy.

So how do you define closure? Or making Amends and moving forward. Being positive and creating a moral definitive is most important currently, looking at your options. It's one step away from going forward. And it's a lot better than fixing what may be wrong. . Returning to the present and dealing with reality is helpful in creating a support system without social biases to deal with.

There is moral justification in this. If you do feel you've gone down the so-called rabbit hole, so to speak, clear your focus. Start with a new view of yourself. And who is actually on your side, This Could give you a new basis and a new start in life You might be surprised with what you get out of it.

THE GAME

This next concept has gotten me thinking for many years. Is life a game? It seems easy to say yes in social realms. What if the concept of there being a game is more useful than not? I found in several situations that someone I respected was asking me that question, and all three times, I thought the person was right. There was no chip on my shoulder. I just considered this idea to be a hypocrisy. It just seemed to me that I would have to draw some line in the sand at some point. But there are a great number of people who do consider it a way to play. Although it does open doors for a realm of experiences to become available to you, I find this to be a venue of education itself. So, to be able to use the game certainly tends to be easier in some ways. The reason is I found that pushing someone away from you is very easy to do even if you don't know the person. Can you imagine what it's like making social contracts with people who are already biased in the beginning? That is if you are in the market for intimacy. In the context of playing a game, I would hope that you get past your disposition to overcome certain social biases. You should know the name of someone, what information he or she is offering, and in what regard the person who is offering takes responsibility for the setting or information that you get. The good thing about playing games is that you always have more opportunities to move forward and don't have obligations. Always know that you're playing with a clean deck of cards and have closure before you get involved with something that may be unorthodox. So, don't be surprised if you wake up one day, and it's no longer a game.

ONE PERSON'S PARADISE IS ANOTHER PERSON'S MISERY

Living in paradise is not just a dream; it is possible. In truth, other than the basics, cuisine, and satire, you could say that you have unlimited use of these things that are available to you. Paradise can be a concept or a combination of different things at the same time. Some people are very extroverted and want to influence some amounts of money other than abstract matter. It depends upon your philosophy. If your lifestyle gives you happiness, you have achieved the dream. It's not about money; it's about the journey. But it's certainly nice to cash in.

Power is position. Position can be a service of responsibility for other people. There is no absence of people who need guidance in this world. Climbing that ladder to reach responsibility for this world is a timeless measure. Educating yourself for the next step in life is an achievement. Having your choice of goals is wisdom. If you don't already live in paradise (almost everybody wants to), it's an actuality that your perception of happiness is the most underrated adventure that you can make. Financial happiness for some people is having an infinite amount of money and resources, although money does not guarantee your happiness. Defined by finances, it may be said that happiness is having all the materialistic things that you want beyond your necessities.

If you rationalize happiness by your finances, it doesn't always work. You have heard the cliché that most people would rather be happier in a shack than be miserable being incredibly wealthy. Unfortunately, the end does not make the means. You could live quite modestly and enjoy what you have rather than continue searching for the wealth that could buy you the next boat. Capitalism is so ingrained in our lives that having money is a very positive thing, but is it worth your happiness? Finding your calling that benefits you financially is the ultimatum that we're all looking for. We, at the same time, do not want to sacrifice our happiness for the short time that we have. This is not to say that we don't want to have our goals. Achieving our goals with having the abundance we want is certainly one of the best answers. The trick is if you do not have a financial plan but have a true calling, keep your eye on the big picture, and you can benefit yourself while doing what you want hedonistically. Always take the time to smell the roses, so to speak. If you have the abstract things in your life that make you comfortable, that's great. The best things in life are free. Being honest about your issues is great and the best policy to resolve them. Including that special person in your life, can be the only thing that you really need. That may be considered paradise. The cost is withheld love.

CREATING YOUR OWN
DESTINY AND PHILOSOPHY

I will give you a list of things that you must not overlook to recover and a way to get all the support, benefits, and help that you need to be able to educate yourself in dealing with the pharmaceutical industry and how they work. Additionally, I will provide all the scientific, therapeutic, and nutritional information that you need to recover. Basically, all the information that I have learned in twelve years of research and the knowledge of all the resources that I've found are in this book and now available to you. At certain points, I will refer you to a different chapter, such as "Troubleshooting." A list at the back of the book shows necessities that you can refer to. There is also a set of pages made to show the steps to making a personal plan to overcome your illness. I can only hope that after you read this book and have the right information, you will know how to execute your plan to be in the best of situations and have advocacy and support other than just your doctor. I cannot express how important advocacy is. Having an agreement to recover can benefit both you and your loved ones, friends, and family.

Everything being what it is, you are the master of your own fate; you create all the possibilities that come your way. If you have an idea, that's the start of creating a goal. If your goal is to be healthier and you create that goal in your mind, you will thrive. If you put yourself in a position that you don't enjoy, it's not just an experience that makes you unhappy; you could have a heart attack, cancer, or worse. If you are lucky enough to find your calling and that special person in your life, that may be all that matters. There is not necessarily a status quo but having the finances to be able to invest in a better life means you have your destiny in your own hands. Living this manifestation is a well-off way to look at the world. This includes your state of mind and your perception of what is. Metaphysics is a search for the truth, and once you acquire the truth, you find that the destiny meant for you, it is within itself yours to believe and use as you wish. Your perception of the truth is having the destiny that you want, and in your perception of that, service is fulfilled.

Philosophy is a way of looking at the world through rose-colored glasses.

There are four levels of enlightenment:

1. Five senses and conceptual thought
2. Materialism and abstract thinking
3. Experience, the hat you wear
4. Your relationships to others
5. Enlightenment, which is having a point of view from the top of the mountain and being responsible for the four points of philosophy

These views can give you your destiny.

Is the glass half full or half empty? The truth is it's always both. The halfway full represents fulfillment, and the half empty represents promise.

Both exist at the same time; what you have to ask yourself is are you really happy?

PERSUASION AND THE IDEAS OF WINNING PEOPLE

The idea of persuasion is to get someone to be motivated to do what you want him or her to do or to understand your point of view. It's a service. This isn't just what you want as a goal. It's the talent of being persuasive. Some people take years to perfect this talent to have an educated guess. There are pros and cons with the idea of persuasion because others are very opinionated. If you pressure people, this tactic does not work most of the time. There are other ways that are more persuasive. You might be in a position of having the need to getting a doctor's care or a lawyer who represents you. If You need to resolve some issue, you need to know that you have the tools to be able to understand and create a sense of promise in your life that can involve other people as well as the power of suggestion. These tools are going to be very important to you at some time in your life.

Some people are in a place where giving less information is better. As an example, if you're in a card game and you're bluffing other people who are apt to call you on the table, you depend on the information you give them. In other cases, like closing a business deal, you might want to show confidence. This all comes down to reading people. Some things sell themselves, like money abstracts or mantras. It's hard to give something for nothing. It shows that you're not as interested in making a deal.

It's worth a good read to see someone else's view. Once you've done that, use your best judgment. You may want to venture an educated guess and see where that gets you. It may be the words people use, their disposition, how they speak, and what they imply. The more you pay attention, the more that you understand, the better you get. It may mean giving up a sizable investment of yourself to close a deal; that's persuasion. These tools will help you to be a breadwinner. Influence and persuasion are goals to have for anyone in sales or business and a good place to start being educated, considering that you might be functionally limited in some way. That doesn't mean that you can't be persuasive and winning is just icing on the cake. You'll know when you get there. Disabled people can be closers as well. Its determined by what you're willing to invest in yourself.

A

MORAL COMPASS AND KNOWING YOURSELF

Moral compass, like attitude, creates your direction. This action defines the difference of right and wrong. In context, it may seem arbitrary, but more people are easily read in this way. Morals create character. Morals define happiness the same way ethics define agreement. If you don't agree, there is no sense of reality, and usually that states that someone is not interested or is in denial. And the way you answer questions controls the direction of the flow of energy. Like creating influence, a good moral compass is a way to start a legacy or a following. Visually, a good moral compass and power is available to you, and if you take that power with you, karma carries you. The truth is available to everyone. Having moral conviction is a state of mind and attitude. You must live with the concept of moral conviction to attain your goals. Moral conviction may be the only answer to having your mental health or regaining it.

You can consider that the truth is who we are as human beings. We are five senses and conceptual thoughts. Knowing the dynamics of who you are will build a future and help you to create a philosophy. And it will help you understand that you have all the tools to complete your goals already. Before we move to an animate situation, we want to go over the idea of a person and who he or she is. I believe that there are all kinds of relationships, family, children, cohorts, people you know and feel that you have a connection with. I have already seen a dog and a deer be best friends. Why? I don't know. I hope that all and any relationships that you have are fulfilling and filled with kindness. Relationships with kindness and respect tend to last longer. Let the small things go and concentrate on what's real and most important. Because having a healthy idea of who you are does help your situation. You may be impaired or have a condition, but that does not mean that you cannot have healthy relationships. Even if you are impaired, this does not mean you are in a social crisis. Consider the value of never having to ask why. Knowing yourself means knowing your virtues, so count your blessings, disabled or not. Character is never a lost endeavor.

GETTING CAPITAL

Yes, even the mentally ill want to be educated and financially well off.

If your idea of paradise is wealth, at least in some minds, it starts with a product or service and hopefully one that sells itself. To start a business, you need a business plan, a budget, and a bottom line. And it may feel as if you've won the lottery. Mercedes convertibles are expensive. Location is everything. You want to go where the money is. There are several ways to get seed money. Once you have a plan, there are ways to submit for a grant if the person you're dealing with has a common interest. You need an education. A master's degree in business isn't just a degree on the wall. It is the knowledge and ability to achieve that bottom line and get into the market that you want. I happened to get into a business that was shut down by a corporate takeover and missed some opportunities that could have made me wealthier. Sometimes there are pros and cons that are out of your control. There are benefits in any business that you may want to get into. A lot of wealthy people are looking for a successful business to invest in. A meal ticket is for most people creating a service that helps you to create finances and float your boat while you're creating the business of your dreams. Credit is extremely important because if you don't treat it right, it could destroy your equity for the future. Everyone is looking for the next big thing, and if you invested in Apple when it was young, you would be wealthy today. Investment-savvy people are people who get ahead by being able to predict the future. Amazon is a great example now.

All these things could produce wealth. Always have an expense/revenue sheet so you don't make a cash cow into a puddle. This doesn't mean that money grows on trees, but if it did, shaking that tree at the right time may be lucrative. I at the height of my illness went back to college and went into business. Buy low; sell high. Money does give you access to the lifestyle you are looking for. Make your choices carefully because it may not be there in the future. My problem was always not knowing how to tie a tie, rather than being filthy rich. I found out that respect for other people paid just as much as a degree. Please remember what I found out, that business builds character. Whether you are functionally well off or not, your health is the best wealth you will ever have. I have had many investors in my life, and I've never lost by investing in that rule.

MAKING A PRESENTATION

Whether you have a condition or not, people are not here to judge you. They're here to see if they can hash out an agreement. If you're lucky enough, this is a good time to be able to make a presentation. It's about your personality, your character, and what you endeavor to do with the life and time that you have on this earth. Accomplishing the impossible is what we hope to achieve every day of our lives to see our dreams come true. Look in the mirror. Look at your clothes, how you carry yourself, your expression, and your disposition. Look at what persona you want to have or portray. We all have a sense of dialogue. If you're talking to a doctor about your health or when you're communicating to make a business deal, be sure that you express your intention and your point of view to make sure the other person gets confirmation. Think out what kind of lifestyle you want and create that lifestyle around yourself. We all have the net ability to conform and recreate ourselves. We create our own reality with persuasion and agreement. Influence may be the greatest tool we have in our toolbox and is one we should consider using much more. Being able to change and evolve is demonstrated by the presentation that we make to others.

Doing these things gives you a game. Anything is possible. Thinking a few steps ahead of another person or group of people will give you the edge to close the deal. Financial or personal balance is easily gained if you already know that you're a winner because winners win.

Intellectually, everything that you create comes back to you. As you evolve, take the steps to increase your health, whatever that might be, whatever goal you might have, financial, personal, or abstract. Clear the cobwebs away from the corners of your room to make sure that you are not inhibited by any distractions and consider your closing. Where you leave your presentation is a great place to reevaluate who you are. Be a perfectionist, and don't cut corners. Always give 110 percent. Even if you have head trauma, the idea of opportunities is always there to create your presentation. Know that you're in a better place because of it. The measure of a person is the way he or she leaves another person feeling. Remember you have nothing to lose and everything to gain by being the best person you can be. Remember that people will respond to your values more than your disposition. It's always a roll of the dice. Don't undercut yourself because you don't feel equal. Always invest and close. Discipline will always tend to win the argument and benefit you personally.

MY SEARCH FOR HELP AND
MY PERSONAL BATTLES

There are several types of schizophrenia. Mine was a paranoid type. My onset was at age nineteen. Some children get the same illness as well. The first thing I did after changing my first medication, which I was allergic to, was to call a friend who paid for my doctor's appointments. Then I moved from where I was living because of the violence there. I would take long walks and get lost. I would run into strangers who tried to help me many times. There was a private hospital I would go to in Oakland, California. My message is that schizophrenia, depression, and PTSD are illnesses that you can recover from, although there are some that are not completely treatable at this time. Even though I am a survivor, the diagnoses that are known for people to not recover from can offer the knowledge and love to give you a better quality of life.

After a list of medications and hospitals, there was no normalcy in my life. What I knew was hallucinations, delusions, and paranoia as well as secondary symptoms. A low percent of people with my condition use Clozaril in the United States. If nothing else, I always considered myself a creationist, meaning my life belonged to God. From 1989 until 2009, I was extremely ill but better every day. The other difference was when I brought nutrition into my life, which I talked about in another chapter. My personal life was dysfunctional, not just from the illness, but from not being able to make a commitment.

One time, I passed out because of my use of Xanax and withdrew for thirty-five days because my doctor was prescribing five tablets a day. That was the worst it got in a hospital system that was dysfunctional to some degree. I thank God for my family who was there for me and the doctors who believed in me when other people didn't. I wish nothing but love and kindness for other people and especially good health. I decided to write this book to help others, considering I have had ten medications, nine hospitalizations, and twenty-five years of conflict. My faith and belief in others and in the world help me to give up any spite that I may have and love people for who they are. Sometimes it's hard to understand people who you don't think are genuine, but that is the true test of the pursuit of happiness itself.

TOLERANCE AND ADDICTION

M edication is helpful to the physical condition if used as directed. Tolerance is used to describe a condition of diminished response to a drug resulting from repeated exposure. I found I was a bit obsessive compulsive and let someone else take over the rendering of my medication. It worked better that way. For some medications, some people feel they want a cleansing of their bodies, every so often when addiction is involved, to resolve the tolerance. Although you should talk to your doctor first, many medications are meant to be used regularly and on a schedule. The beauty of medications is that some of them can be resolved by substitutes, such as vitamins or nutrition, or in a holistic direction. These answers can be useful at the same time if not helpful. People generally have their own idea of cleansing their bodies.

If you listen to your doctor, he or she might never tell you about cleaning your physical state of being. The division and use should be the point of your feeling the effectiveness of the medication that you're prescribed, although doctors will tell you that if you miss a dose of medication, you can take the dose the next time it's available without throwing off your physical state. The question is does it dispute the effectiveness of the use of medications that are prescribed? Listen to your doctor. You also have the right to choose a different physician. If you feel its necessary Yes, you have an option. If someone in your home or family wants to do a cleansing, it may be a matter of a personal ritual or agreement.

To deal with addiction, it may be a matter of agreement with your doctor and the medication that you take. Any substitutes of drugs that don't belong in your body should be resolved immediately, and you should plan with your doctor to make sure that your cleansing is done in an effective way. Therefore, we have structure in our lives—it doesn't have to be painful to do a cleansing. The well-being of our lives is not necessarily at risk. Now we are in a time with drugs like fentanyl being laced into illicit drugs sold on the market. In fact, it's known that 75,000 people died this way in 2020—twice the number who died of the flu. I lost a cousin to this in spring of 2021. The bottom line is that quality of life has rules in regard to our beliefs and physical state. This is worth talking about. Remember that a man on a cross is a symbol of our culture and the resurrection of our souls. Again, neglect is a crime to me. The cohesion of the fabric of our society is balanced by this effect. Remember that it's your choice to educate yourself, evolve, and adapt to your values and choose neither neglect nor reckless endangerment. If you are using a drug that has side effects that you cannot bear, or you are addicted to a chemical that is not healthy, pursuing a different path is extremely important. Being able to educate yourself into a healthier way of life is or should be your priority. Know that illegal use of drugs can cause disease or affliction that you may not be able to bear or live with, including effects on your mental health and institutionalization.

There is a silent pandemic. There are tens of thousands of people in institutions in the United States and more in other countries in the world. You must understand that these people in the world are human beings who have been neglected by science. These people suffer from illnesses that can be treated, but unfortunately society tends to treat these people as second-class citizens. They should at least be given health, nutrition, and a right to follow their religious choice. Unfortunately, unless they're in a private hospital, they are treated as a minority and denied these basic rights. These illnesses can be treated with the right meds and nutrition, and can be educated against and outsourced. These are people of our own family trees who are overlooked. Other than their personal needs, recovery could be pushed forward. This is a $300-billion-a-year industry with human beings who have done nothing wrong and can be considered consumers of a broken health-care system. They are denied some benefits, such as nutrition, their religious beliefs, and the free enterprise system, everything we take for granted. The majority of people that stay in institutions for more time than they should be there. Recovery and housing, meeting the basic needs of people, will save the country tens of billions of dollars in revenue. Programs like these are said to be necessary to change the abilities of others and help turn them into functional, fulfilling, prosperous people, although I feel they fall short.

The question is can you put a price on these people's lives? This is the silent pandemic, which is a cancer in our country; it reminds you how many people are mentally ill. In this country, it is time to care for our own families and let freedom be a constitutional right available to them. These people can no longer be discarded with prejudice. They are worthwhile human beings. They belong in their own homes. This form of human trafficking is intolerable and unacceptable.

If we are denied these basic rights, we create an undefined and unresolved minority.

Treating people like cattle should be banned legally in this country. It's wrong to institutionalize people before we give them the structure, the stability, and the best health care available to them. The real rule here is don't judge other people before you judge yourself. As people in charge of these contemptuous views, we want to honor our Constitution and religious beliefs. We must choose a mental health-care system that is inclusive of our families and health. We have a moral responsibility to represent our families with a judge present, or we deny our families of their freedoms and liberties. We must have human values and educate people so that this practice is no longer in use. You can restore your mental health with psychiatry, therapy, and nutrition and better yourself and others. You have to remember that it is not your fault that you have a mental illness but rather pick a time to choose your battles and continue to believe in your real dreams. This is not a misunderstood illness but a future for our country. It's our responsibility to decide what that future is and educate one another. I call this the silent pandemic.

PHILOSOPHY OF RELATIONSHIPS

You can make any deal or social contract or negotiate in any relationship, that you want. In a partnership, you have ultimate goals that you both agree upon as being the best. Partnerships are 100 percent rather than both being 50 percent for two people, and that creates surplus in many areas. Let's think about one person having taken on responsibility for both sides of the relationship. It's those sets of regards, like a gentleman walking a lady across the street, a gentleman opening a door, and so on. In reality, it is a set of values and a set of agreements to be loyal to set forward to accomplish and cohabitate in a lifestyle.

I want to tell you a story about an old friend I had who was worth $90 million and looking for a relationship. Unfortunately, he had a bad back and could literally not get out of bed. And every single woman wanted him at least for his money and his charisma, and that was all that happened. So, what kind of diamond in the rough do you think you will really have? If you really value yourself, maybe someone else will too. Consider someone's value and virtues before you get into a relationship and know what you're getting into. Sometimes there will be a deal breaker in your relationship, and you must value those things that you think are important to you and even negotiate in some situations. Meal tickets are easy to come by, but do you really want to include that person in your life? Think about what you're including. If you're in a relationship that's meant to be, fate will conquer all and any conclusion to that relationship, which will happen without you having to do anything about it other than be at cause. The glass is always half full and half empty. You must find your own level. We all make personal choices. Remember to be true to yourself. Love conquers all.

LIVING IN THE PRESENT

I found out that I was hiding who I truly was. I started to estimate when I would die, which is a morbid topic. Nonetheless, I realized that I could live to be one hundred years old. I also realized that I had many issues that were somewhere in the back of my head. So, what's the real explanation? How does time affect us, and how do hidden issues affect us? First, we'll try to not deal with time at all, which is easy for me because I'm a freelance writer, although many people have nine-to-five jobs. You don't have a way to control time. The minutes turn into days, the days into months, and the months into years. There's nothing wrong with having a schedule. And some people are better off with a certain amount of structure. I've heard that you can be healthier outside of the home than inside. It's a choice to make. It's nice to have finances, even if it doesn't buy you love. There's a lot that it does get you.

Nonetheless time tends to be an idea that we obligate ourselves to. Again, if you do live in comparison to abstract things or science that we need to survive, live to a hundred, look back, and ask yourself what is important to you, the answer would be the people you love, meaning it wasn't different anytime you got off that plane in a different time zone. This means that love and the people you share life with are most important. Including having respect and boundaries, you must consider your priorities and know someone personally before you make any investments with the person. We are all wired in some way. All these ideals only exist functionally in life because we make the choices we do deliberately. The better you communicate and just focus on the basic things, like attention and goals, the better chance you give yourself of getting to live in the present. Don't compare the people you spend time with in your life to each other. Giving your obligations away only means that you live in the present without obstacles. You can reset your mind constantly, and it's a good idea. The earlier you agree to a set of goals, the better off you are. You are putting yourself in a position of knowing who you are and how you relate to other people. Reality is based on present time and the people you spend that time with. We're not comparing apples with oranges. Having a condition does not mean that you will not have a way to live in the present; there's no way not to. This is a freeing thought. Einstein said time is an illusion. The illusion is that time tends to stand still, which creates the idea of the present. The truth is that the world is ever evolving.

OUR PERCEPTION
OF OURSELVES

Our bodies are all connected, but our perception changes around the idea of good and bad circumstances. Psychology tells us that perception is those processes of rational and emotional thinking. This is a difficult question to ask but may be necessary.

Through our behavior that we base our lives upon, the way we think, and the way we perceive this world, we all endeavor to resolve our issues. Although the destination we seek is no different in the way that we create the experiences that we search for, we reward our endeavors and create the idea of the work that we do. Is there a way that we decide on our direction? Or do we justify our ideas to access our aesthetic values? I struggled with my own sense of judgment over myself for years. I always blamed myself or someone else for my condition. So next, we must understand the circumstances that represent our health and how they affect us. We judge our lives by looking at the most painful experiences or the most positive ones. The same is true about people in need of support and how we show them the beneficial ideas in the world. The real question is how do we perceive ourselves and our world? So what is real or a complex paradox, reality or dream? We may agree on one idea and not another. Our perception is the human condition—how we choose what we believe and why. If this is the question of the human apparatus that we live with, it is the same with our health. In many ways, we seek positive experiences. The better that we feel, the better the quality of life we lead. Take a moment to find ways to give away your pain if only for a moment. Forgiveness of yourself is just as powerful as the remote idea that you may or may not have acceptance or approval around yourself or in your consciousness.

That's right. I'm telling you to give yourself a break regularly, like every hour of your life. The less you confine yourself, the better you feel about your state of mind. People live in the same realm of existence in this world. Give yourself a way off the hook that you might have put yourself on. No one has power over you other than the power you give them. Remembering this idea can move mountains, and it's much healthier than the confines of misery we sometimes endeavor to believe.

THE SPIRAL STAIRCASE
AND FEELING LIMITED

This idea or concept is as stated: you go up every step and get closer to prosperity, answer, or agenda. Even if you evolve to any self-regret, don't worry; you can always start over. At the top of the staircase, you will be called to elevate or support yourself at that level. And there is a necessity to be there. It has purpose and measure, more than what you make it out to be. It is putting your foot forward and pushing on to have a responsibility for life. This is often called success or a safe place to take responsibility for yourself or state of mind. At the top, you own that place because you know it serves a purpose. You become the light of the ocean that protects the sea. This is your identity and principal allure. Everyone serves a purpose; some just haven't found that lighthouse. We're only as limited as we make ourselves; some of us have just not found our calling yet.

When my own doctors suggested that I write this book, there was an incident in a downstairs room where my doctor worked, where he was going to another location, and he confided in me. I have a box full of three things that I value in my life. In this box, there were three things: a picture, a letter, and a bottle of fish oil. He said he was taking all his belongings with him in a very small box. At first, I thought he was just being humorous, and then I realized he was quite truthful. The three things he valued were in this small box.

Most of us feel limited with just having a mental illness. It's a terrible illness to go through. No one wants to have these kinds of illnesses. There are way too many problems already in the world. Because of these problems that don't seem to be going away, in progression, I have the good news to tell you that because of the personalities or semantics in this world, you may not want to take chances. So, in giving up our better judgments, there are three relevant elements to think about: attention, good listening, and agreements. These are the three tools that will lead to opening doors in your life. This particular doctor based his life on the conversations with the people he met, with conditions or not. Those conversations meant more to him that any diagnosis. There are pros and cons in life. Attention and kindness are part of life. Regard yourself as a patron, and let God decide. You can know that it's not due to your illness; it is the same for everyone. Here, some people are better readers than others, especially if they are the ones who make the decisions in life. But I've never met a person who doesn't fall into social phobias occasionally when it's not his or her call to make. Remember we own our own limitations, so don't judge yourself too quickly; you may just be facing the truth when God is watching.

THE CIRCUMSTANCES WITH MENTAL ILLNESS

L iving with a mental illness through the coronavirus has been like a double whammy. This is how psychiatrists and caregivers have become invaluable.

In the coronavirus era, I was lucky to find a friend who was interested in talking once a week, which is wonderful. Although I was interested in the attention that she gave me, I came on too strong. But in the fourth week, we became friends—at least that was my interpretation. The best advice I got was not to get emotionally involved. And how could I in such a limited state?

My feeling in general was that I had found her to be attractive and talented. But my belief is that it can only bring me more faith regarding life. I play by the rules. It is beautiful to be able to live at home with my family. It did help me focus better. In my life, it seemed that we would all have choices to make with our lifestyles. And although I was able to get in touch with people who were on the front lines fighting this virus, reality in this era makes its own way. Functionally, we tragically only have the distance we have and are here while this virus is around. We don't have more than the limits we impose on ourselves. Yet not being ill is a thousand times better than lost love. The amount that we present ourselves as a social society gives us a relative respect for life, although at the end of the day, it comes down to belief, health, and resolve.

Unfortunately, some circumstances we are not in control of. I would have given her away if there was a better life for her, and I did. Being a gentleman or being in a relationship that had no purpose or honor made no sense to me in this case.

One of the two things that will happen in this situation is dealing with my false pride or dealing with a sense of responsibility. There is no choice to make. No one in this world is obligated to do what others might expect of them. Life might be a roll of the dice, so have common sense and be careful what you ask for. Again, don't get too emotionally involved. Know that head trauma might be what you deal with after your psychosis, and you're better off for it. Admit that you have no control over a situation and let someone else take that responsibility from you. This is what will help you the most. In a world of best wishes, people who are resourceful are willing to say when they are beaten. That is how doctors became well off in the first place, taking away the responsibilities from others at a time when there seemed to be only futility. This is an extremely informational idea that should live on and has great worth.

OBLIGATIONS, MENTAL ILLNESS, AND HUMANITY

B elieving in myself as an artist is one of the assurances that helped me be as creative as I wish, and I've never met an artist on a deadline.

You're not obligated to do anything you do not want to do, mentally ill or not. This is the rule. We tend to give in to our social values for love. Because of this, if it does not bring us happiness, it may not be the right subject; it may be the way we look at that goal. It may be difficult when you have harder days rather than better days but putting obligations on top of the life or subject you intend to make only makes life more difficult. My goal was for better health, and so I did do everything to get to be where I am. I listened to over forty doctors and found out the tricks of the trade. The better the ideas I tended to come up with, the fewer obligations in my life I felt. Knowing that there were obligations in life just made me happier to work not on the clock, with support that I could know and enjoy. Here's the trick about obligations: it's only the lesser of the obligation and the better reward. If the subject is attainable, learn all you can about it, and then plan on how to achieve your goals without obligations. Your dreams can be attainable if you're willing to be patient and search for the truth.

I did find some comfort in knowing the state of New York has a privacy law and that my health records were sealed.

Discretion must be coupled with humane actions. Don't give up even one inch of regard for your moral compass. It can cost you or destroy relationships. It doesn't matter what kind of circumstance you are in, if you don't take responsibility for your actions, it is a destitute place to be in life. You should render yourself without that responsibility and let someone who is confident and educated take it on. Have a healthy regard toward others in life and take that responsibility if a sanctuary is needed or if someone is ill or in need of medical care. I realized that I was obsessive and asked a family member to take control of my medications at times. Currently, with so many STDs, there must be a solvent way of regarding your safety with the responsibility to continue to be healthy, which means to be tested before having any kind of sexual activity. Make sure that you truly have personal feelings for someone before you bare yourself to him or her. Any kind of intimate situation means being safe, comfortable, and caring for the person that you share your human side or intimacy with. I learned this early in life.

I was once diagnosed with HIV in a clinic that had blood draws, and one month later, they called me back in to say they had made a mistake. To my surprise, this scared me straight. To this day, I have no STDs to my name. This way, you are safe and easily allow love. Be tested first, use protection, and you don't have to wonder. I did feel badly for the other person who got the diagnosis that was in place of mine.

BAD HABITS AND ONE THING AT A TIME

realized that if you're on the road to recovery for any diagnosis, you can set back your recovery several years by using any kind of street drugs for any amount of time. There is a point where you can reach rock bottom. If you find yourself in this condition, there is no alternative but survival. The priority is that everyone has regard for others, and we make our appointments. The only good thing about the dark place that you're in is that there is no place but up. Usually, as the health system renders itself, you must sign a form called a 2120, meaning that you will cause no harm to yourself or anyone else. You can consider working toward a PhD and see what other business offers are on the table. This is a place to understand how to reconcile the pain or hurt caused by the situation that you may be in. I believe in creating your own destiny but in being constructive to have an amicable way of life. Closure and resolve may be the best answers in your toolbox at this time. Each person must be considered an asset and a liability, and these two concepts bring promise to life. Be sure to not involve anyone who could be a bad influence in your life and decide to involve yourself in a better future and environment. Be deliberate. Find a sense of direction to better yourself. There is always time to change your habits and patterns, so don't pressure yourself too much. Set up a better lifestyle for yourself deliberately. Find all the things in life that can benefit you, and put your best foot forward as you try to effect changes in your life.

I took this time in my life to make amends. Once you have forgiven yourself, give the same to others. You will find they appreciate you more.

COMPLETING GOALS, FOCUS, AND DEALING WITH INTROVERTS

f or when you find yourself in a situation where you have no revenue or you are in a situation where considering your future is the best course or the only course to take, remember that love and family come first, and other people may have the assets to help you. Consider that you have the idea or a list of goals to make. This is possibly a great thing to do. Restoring your sense of self is a property of life and focus. Setting a list of goals to focus on can make you effective and better able to go into a place where you can attain value in yourself, along with hope, courage, and dignity. A list of things you aspire to will help to fulfill your regard for life. Understand that true intention and a genuine way of life make a statement. There are always other people in the same boat as you are, and there are always other ways to help you achieve a basic way to define your needs. Setting goals and having focus will help you to do this. These two concepts will be beneficial to you and others.

(Make a list of goals for yourself here.)

Bettering yourself involves reading people and knowing how to trust others and how to make better sense of their ideas and concepts to build on. Trust is the best way to create structure in any sense. Remember that ego and pride are only lost and will not help your cause. This is a time to help yourself and create personal gain.

I had a friend I was renting out a room to who was extremely introverted.

Most introverts show a sensitivity about leaving their comfort zone. They are often more interested in their hobbies and do not care about their personal selves. They lack inspiration, and they tend to absolve themselves of any personal responsibility no matter the situation they may be in. To resolve their sense of identity, finding a way to reason with them often works. We must find a way to help them realize that there is a consideration to the material things that they want. Show them they can have a new car, new clothes, or a new suit, and money can increase or change their lifestyle. This shows that education will help them play for a position in this world. Focused attention and a title mean worth in this world. Show them that equity is value, as is the responsibility that comes with it. The respect and regard for the benefit of having material things can be far more important than the little effort that they would have to put into taking on a small amount of that responsibility, and that is the minimal risk that they would take to attain it. Huge amounts of material goods and influence over other people might get them interested in these ideas. The more you invest in them, the more revenue they will acquire. Every introverted person who has an interest in our economy is a new way to take a new set of values and make that set of values a new type of currency.

APPROVAL AND ACKNOWLEDGMENT

Friendships are born out of this two-way street. Anyone who has something to say has that ability to make the world his or hers. Good genetics and a viable regard for life's answers are available on this impasse. So social gain is important when you believe in someone else. I've found that these two tools are the best two social answers you have in your arsenal—not that it is just flattering; it's very beautiful to make someone have a better day. We don't have a lot of social gain in these trying times, so try to ask for absolutely nothing back. I've always believed unconditional love is something that you don't see very often or only in close family circles, but it comes in other forms, sometimes as one of those things you say when you invite someone into your family.

A close friend of mine said to me on my birthday that I was a good man. This remark just turned me around and made me feel as if I were talking to others about a rainbow that had passed by me in the most beautiful of rain showers in the year. I tend to believe women always seek out approval the same way that men wait for acknowledgment. They seem to come far and few between unless you have a great deal of faith in your family or at the dinner table. Love seems to come true one in a hundred times, and love and intimacy can't be bought. This is the reality I know to be true—if you do make vows at a confirmation, you have these tools every day in your lifetime.

Approval and acknowledgement are available in certain situations. There are two things to consider here: first, that you are in the right platform for the aspect of these situations to be relevant, and second, that you have an understanding that the social values of another person are open to understanding and that the consideration is openly viewed as polite manners. Life is worth celebrating in good moderation.

NEW BEGINNINGS

began to study psychology as a hobby several years ago. It is not entirely defined until there is a hypothesis you want to test. No one lives on a desert island alone. No one survives alone in this world. The determined factor in this case is that it takes two people to bring a life into this world, and love or relationships are the same way. A gain of leverage or social power to engage in the rule of two leaves nobody incomplete. You may understand abstract ideas or complexities but not love alone. And nobody has a right to take a person and do more than identify the personality of someone with the power of two and have the result of human contact or procreation. We evolved in the power of one and are absolved in the power of two. Human nature is not neglect. As much as nature affects us, we neglect by the falsehood of the power of one, not two, and are all our own creation. This is the rule of personalities, and this is how we attend to people who are only responsible for themselves. This encompasses the maturity of moral respect for others. To develop one set of ideas, this genesis is called maturity in a state of mind or virtue. It encompasses our honor or discrimination in the way that we communicate. We mentor our families with this compass and the true assets of the value of self rather than that of mind and body. The personalities, we are conditioned to believe, are the power of two not one. These personalities are anatomically correct to the point of one as stated and as per one to four. Who you are is demonstrated in the id, which was pointed out by Freud. It seems to be independent but incudes the identity of that which we know to be who we are. The power of one can be explained only by the lack of discrimination, which equals the value of humanity. Personality is why we attend and discriminate. I will address human behavior in the chapter on humanities. The four personality types are pragmatic, choleric, sanguine, and melancholy.

THE RECOVERY PLAN

You must remember that your health is the most important goal you will ever attain in your life. Make a list of the assets of your health care here. With this list, you will start your recovery. This is a list of basic therapy.

1. Get the benefits that are available to you.
2. Take care of yourself and your surroundings.
3. Be able to define and plan for the financial part of your life and well-being.
4. Get the best care for yourself, medically and psychologically.
5. Know you have the best medication available to you.
6. Have the best plan for your nutrition, including vitamins and a healthy diet.
7. Have a responsible relationship with your doctors or care workers.
8. Have a social or networking plan to help you have humane contact with others.
9. Use nutrition to balance your well-being and your body so you can fight off a virus or infection.

Copying a list with these eight goals and checking them off will help you to recover to your best health. This list is extremely important and should be read weekly.

True philanthropy is giving a person back his or her life and not caring about making money in the process.

Pages of Recovery Plan

Page1 Ageement with your Dr

Page2 Médications

Page3 Nutritional Product

Page4 Support System

Page5 Challenging your Brain

Page6 Psychosocial Rules

Page7 Troubleshooting

THE COMPLEX BRAIN

The complex brain is built upon an incredible number of diversities. The brain that we are told we only use 10 percent of, according to Johns Hopkins, creates a city of neurotransmitters, neuropathways, and microprocessors that control our human functions and our intellect. This has put us at the top of the food chain and created human communication abilities and a world of ideology that has not even been discovered.

If you can, imagine a world that has expanded to such a degree that we have gone into space, split the atom, discovered the human genome, and created a world of imagination from just where you sit.

Unfortunately, people around the world are still dying of illness and famine. I believe that this has a lot to do with how we perceive the world. We are so busy looking forward that we have neglected to focus on the issues that are right in front of us. With all our great achievements, pain and affliction should be unnecessary, unless you believe that this is the destiny of the human condition. I don't believe that. What I do believe is that we could eradicate many of the ills of our current society if we would just give them a priority and stop fighting among ourselves. It may be easy to look outward into the world and know the brain as we understand it. We are not using our resources to adjust to the human condition or resolve the health and functionality of our brain because our perception and intellect precede our view of what a functional mind means. In other words, we must teach ourselves to adapt. Adjusting our own perception of ourselves may be the real answer regarding the world as we understand it.

The world can and will change in a lot of cases of mental illness, which can be curable. Just like we recreate our view of the world, not just in our own perception, we can literally recreate ourselves and change our values and our viewpoints. As we manifest our destinies, we can cure and recreate our lives and the health of our brain chemistry. I believe in a limitless idea of life rather than living within the bounds of a set diagnosis.

Realms of the perception of a better life are at our doorsteps.

Printed in the United States
by Baker & Taylor Publisher Services